3.12.93.

For Matthew Burns

at the Brother

[signature, illegible]

AN ELEGY IN ARCADY:
An Artist's View of
Housman's Poetry

AN ELEGY IN ARCADY:

An Artist's View of Housman's Poetry

Written and illustrated by
Piers Browne

Second Edition
1990

ASHFORD
SOUTHAMPTON

Published by Ashford
1 Church Road
Shedfield
Hampshire SO3 2HW

First published in 1989
This revised edition published in 1990

British Library Cataloguing in Publication Data

An Elegy in Arcady: An Artist's View of Housman's Poetry, 2nd ed.
Browne, Piers
1. Poetry in English. Housman, A. E.
(Alfred Edward), 1859–1936. Shropshire lad
I. Title
821'. 912

ISBN 1-85253-230-0

Title page illustration: IN ARCADIA, from the etching by
Adriaan Frans Boudwyns

Typeset in 11/13 pt Palatino by Acorn Bookwork, Salisbury, Wiltshire
Printed by Hartnolls Limited, Bodmin, Cornwall, England

To Char, my wife, and Natasha,
Christopher and Kate

Where the apple reddens,
Never pry –
Lest we lose our Edens,
Eve and I.

Robert Browning, *A Woman's Last Word*

It is and it must in the long run be
better for a man to see things as
they are than to be ignorant of them.

A. E. Housman, Introductory Lecture at
University College, London 1892

Contents

List of Illustrations   viii

Acknowledgements   x

Introduction   xii

1 · Ubi Nunc Arcadia?   1

2 · Housman's Life and Career   8

3 · The Craft of Romance: Local and Latin
Influences   41

4 · Hardy, Sappho, the Rubáiyát and Stars   86

5 · Shropshire: The Naming of Arcadia   121

6 · Valediction: The Great Truths   148

Bibliography   163

Illustrations

In Arcadia   *title page*

The Arcadian Shepherds   *facing page 4*

View of Dordrecht   *facing page 5*

Housman, aged 35 and at 63   *facing page 20*

View towards the Clee Hills   *between pages 20 and 21*

The Reading Room in the British Museum   *between pages 20 and 21*

Moses Jackson   *facing page 21*

Housman at 51   *facing page 36*

The Seed Roller   *between pages 36 and 37*

Great Court, Trinity College   *between pages 36 and 37*

Avenue of Cherry Trees   *facing page 37*

Homer and Aeschylus   *facing page 52*

Landscape   *between pages 52 and 53*

Valley of Vision   *between pages 52 and 53*

Housman aged 67   *facing page 53*

In the Welsh Marches   *facing page 68*

Venice   *between pages 68 and 69*

Olives   *between pages 68 and 69*

The Severn at Buildwas   *facing page 69*

Firdowsi and his Fellow Tenth-century Poets   *facing page 84*

Cornfield by Moonlight   *between pages 84 and 85*

St Augustine in his Study   *between pages 84 and 85*

Man and Woman Gazing at the Moon   *facing page 85*

'Whispering' Aspen   *facing page 100*

The Long Mynd   *between pages 100 and 101*

An Arcadia: Wensleydale   *between pages 100 and 101*
'Team Ploughing'   *facing page 101*
'Falling' Stream   *facing page 116*
Ludlow   *between pages 116 and 117*
'Labouring' Highway   *between pages 116 and 117*
'Standing' Hill   *facing page 117*
Adam and Eve in Paradise   *facing page 132*
The Wrekin at Sunset   *facing page 133*

· Acknowledgements

Further to specific acknowledgements in chapter notes, the author and publisher would particularly like to thank the following for permission to reproduce copyright material: the Society of Authors as the literary representative of the Estate of A. E. Housman, and Jonathan Cape Ltd, publishers of *The Collected Poems of A. E. Housman*, for extracts from his published writing © 1989 including those in *The Letters of A. E. Housman*, first published Rupert Hart Davis Ltd and Harvard University 1971, and Granada Publishing Ltd; extracts from the Introductory Lecture (October 1892) and The Name and Nature of Poetry (May 1933) from *A. E. Housman Selected Prose*, ed. John Carter (CUP, 1961); and for extracts from The Inaugural Lecture (May 1911) – The Confines of Criticism (CUP, 1969) ed. John Carter; the Lilly Library, Indiana University, the University of Illinois Library, the Syndics of the Fitzwilliam Museum, the Library of Trinity College Cambridge, the Library of University College, London, and the British Museum, for material from their collection of Housman's letters; the Manuscript Division of the Library of Congress and the Board of the British Library for extracts from the diaries of A. E. Housman; the Master and Fellows of Magdalene College, Cambridge, for an extract from the diaries of A. C. Benson; *The Listener* for a line from Prof. D. Shackleton Bailey; and Doubleday & Co., New York, for an extract from T. E. Lawrence's *The Seven Pillars of Wisdom*. Finally my thanks to Michael D. Reeve the present Kennedy Professor of Latin at Cambridge for some elucidation concerning the popularity of the Classical Tripos at Cambridge University, and to the late Mr Tressilian Nicholas, formerly senior bursar of Trinity, for divulging his reminiscences concerning A. E. Housman.

Regarding the illustrations and small extracts from Housman's letters in the text, I would like to thank John Pugh, the Housman Society, and the Society of Authors, London.

I owe a debt of gratitude to the cheerful and expert typing of two patient people, Doreen Porter and Ann Coulson, both brilliant emendators of illegible texts. My thanks also extend to Tom Robinson for proofreading and to Martin Noble for editing what was a more rustic ramble than I here offer the gentle reader.

ABBREVIATIONS USED IN THE TEXT

ASL	*A Shropshire Lad*	1st edn 1896
LP	*Last Poems*	1st edn 1922
MP	*More Poems*	1st edn 1936
AP	*Additional Poems*	1st edn 1937

Jonathan Cape Ltd in this country have frequently reprinted collections of all Housman's published poetry; *Complete Poems*, ed. Basil Davenport and Tom Burns Haber was published by Henry Holt & Co., 1959, in a Centennial Edition in the United States of America.

Most lines of poetry quoted in the text are fragments taken from whole poems as is necessary to make a point – a practice which might, even in these circumstances, have considerably annoyed Housman.

Introduction

I spent many years of my life recreating *A Shropshire Lad*, that is, illustrating nearly every poem and setting each letter of each word of each poem by hand, ready for printing. Both processes were extremely time-consuming. Slowly, too, the need grew to become better acquainted with the poet and discover his motivation for writing such beautiful, wistful poetry. Strangely, there is a blind spot in my memory as to the point at which I made the decision to write about Housman. From what little I knew about him, his affection for the human race seemed so thin, so selective that at first I was repulsed. Yet, through his poems, my curiosity led me to approach him.

I chose the enigmatic title of this book because, while 'ashes to ashes, dust to dust' could be called Housman's chant, 'loveliest of trees' was certainly his canticle. It is that combination of landscape and sadness which excited me to put pen to paper and write an appreciation of Housman and especially his song. Also, since Epicurus – whose ideas Housman often shared – once wrote in his famous garden in Athens that 'death matters neither to the living nor to the dead', I found that that sort of philosophic utterance provoked the philosopher in me to express disagreement.

In this second edition I have been fortunate to improve that which I had without doubt previously stated in a manner more haphazard than any Greek philosopher would have dared to proffer.

Piers Browne
Wensleydale, 1990

1 · UBI NUNC ARCADIA?

Fortunatus et ille deos qui novit agrestis

Fortunate too is the man who has come to know the gods of the countryside

Virgil, *Georgics* ii, line 493

The ancients at least knew what they wanted in art, and we do not.

Matthew Arnold, *Preface to First Edition of Poems* (1853)

The notion of an earthly paradise is embedded deep in the collective psyche of mankind: rumours of its existence have been a persistent feature in the literature and mythology of the world since prehistoric times. Moses was apparently in his 120th year when, from Mount Nebo (or Pisgah), he saw that greatest of 'promised lands', the second Garden of Eden. Although Judaism invokes a paradise never to be reached, it is significant that 'garden' and 'paradise' are the same word in Persian and Arabic. For a walled garden was a sanctuary, and especially so for royalty who could wander about in it, their one safe haven, their 'paradise', built, regrettably often, on the bones of other human beings. The Indians find such beauty on earth in the Vishnu Purāna, while for the Persians it is in their sacred book the Bundahish. Indeed the Persian Zoroaster, whose beliefs held sway for over a thousand years until the rise of Islam, spoke of Mount Damavand as being both a heavenly and earthly paradise. The Chinese spurned the fiery (literally) zeal of Zoroastrianism in the seventh century although to this day, many Chinese ignore abstract deities and worship gods of the soil, rivers and hills, wind and rain and so on.

While Christians should know that paradise is not an earthly place but a state of being where worship is offered, scholars have tried to locate the biblical Garden of Eden in the Book of Genesis – 'The Lord God planted a garden eastward in Eden'[1] – in the plain of the Euphrates around Babylon or the land, about two hundred miles south in countryside of similar historical and archaeological interest. Whereas Cain's 'land of Nod' was too far east of Eden, Milton placed paradise just east of Eden and described the Arcadian profusion of 'hill and dale and plain' which Satan, perched like a cormorant on the Tree of Life, could see spread before him.[2] Even in the late books of the Old Testament, the Hebrew word *pardes*, consistent with its Greek counterpart, παράδειθος, meaning Paradise, crops up three times in relation to three different geographical locations. Certainly in Christian and Judaic religions, 'original sin' destroyed the Garden of Eden, the Earthly paradise, so that all that remained for the concept of 'paradise' to occupy was one of the poles of transcendental existence, with 'inferno' as its polar opposite.

The classical Greek Arcadia, a modern transliteration is present day Arkhadia, was, in contrast, specifically located in the mountainous region of the central Peloponnesus. The pastoral purity of Arcadian life perhaps explains why it was represented as a paradise in Greek and Roman bucolic poetry and why the idea of an Arcadia, rooted both in classical art and history, has persisted in European art from the literature of the Renaissance until the twentieth century – pre-eminently in the modern era, as I shall show, in the poems of A. E. Housman.

The lesser god Daphnis is said to have been a Sicilian shepherd whose father was Hermes the herald –

the Roman god Mercury. He was taught to play the flute by Pan and is credited with being the father of bucolic poetry. But it is Theocritus (310–250 BC) who in reality was the creator of the pastoral form in poetry. Born in Syracuse which was founded as a Greek colony in south-eastern Sicily, his poems were called *eidyllia* (idylls), which is a diminutive of *eidos* (image), and possibly means 'little poems'. His surviving poems include bucolics and mimes, which are set in the country, as well as epics, lyrics and epigrams, set in towns.

Theocritus's originality in portraying characters as real countryfolk made him famous, even during his lifetime, in the eastern Mediterranean. Earlier the tragic poet Euripides had also presented his heroes and heroines not as they ought to have been but as they were. But Theocritus had a light touch; he mixed his gods in small doses. Famed for his thirty-one short idylls, number VIII features a song contest between 'the gentle herdsman', Daphnis, and Menalcas, a musical Sicilian shepherd. An unnamed goatherd is roped in to judge them and, after much banter and two songs, Daphnis is declared the victor. In the previous idyll ('Harvest-Home'), Theocritus paints a portrait, warts, reeking goatcoat and all, of another goatherd, a devout Arcadian who, incidentally, one can still sight in Mediterranean lands today:

Slung o'er his shoulder was a ruddy hide
Torn from a he-goat, shaggy, tangle-haired,
That reeked of rennet yet: a broad belt clasped
A patched cloak round his breast, and for a staff
A gnarled wild-olive bough his right hand bore.[3]

The lyrical and elegaic poems of Theocritus and his near contemporary Callimachus were imitated two hundred years later by Roman poets, especially

Propertius and Catullus. Virgil, the 'great mediator between the antique and ancient world',[4] aimed in *The Bucolics* to transport Theocritus's shepherds into what is now the land of Italian farmers. He thus created shepherds who were neither Theocritan nor true to life, and yet this is perhaps part of their charm. Theocritus was not interested in plumbing the depths of the human condition but was refreshing in his lively, witty and down-to-earth loquaciousness. By the eighteenth century the liberties that had been taken with the form prompted Samuel Johnson to remind us that

> If we search the writings of Virgil for the true definition of Pastoral, it will be found in a poem in which any action or passion is represented by its effects upon a country life. Whatever therefore may, according to the common course of things, happen in the country may afford a subject for a pastoral poem.

At the same time he lashed out at the loose standards of contemporary versifiers, announcing that poor old Daphne and Thyrsis had had enough. More and more fatuity had been crammed into their mouths by more and more popinjays,

> who filled their productions with mythological allusions, with incredible fictions and with sentiments which neither passion nor reason could have dictated, since the change which religion has made in the whole system of the world.

Virgil, who may have 'mediated' between the antique and ancient worlds, had no chance of perceiving the affinity between poetry and religion which the Christian faith has inspired, and could still write:

4

THE ARCADIAN SHEPHERDS, from the painting by Nicholas Poussin (*by permission of the Trustees of the Chatsworth Collection*)

VIEW OF DORDRECHT, from the painting by Aelbert Cuyp (*reproduced by courtesy of the Trustees of the National Gallery, London*)

> Yet sing this song
> Upon your hills, Arcadians! none but ye
> Can sing.[5]

Indeed the Arcadians seem to have sung their pagan song longest, for it is a fact that the metamorphosis of Zeus into the figure of Christ, as witnessed in their statuary, took longer in the southern district of Peloponnesus than anywhere else in Greece.

Early in the Renaissance the form was revived by Petrarch (1304–74) and later by Politian (1454–94). But it was the Neapolitan poet Jacopo Sannazaro (1458–1530) whose *Arcadia* (1485) was to influence the English poet Sir Philip Sidney to write his pastoral romance *Arcadia* (1577–80, revised 1580–4), a prose work interspersed with lyrics. Sidney's *Arcadia* came to embody the main themes of Arcadia for the next few hundred years. A golden world of innocent shepherds and shepherdesses is combined with a sterner world of violent action that for me is less real than the Theocritan original.

Although it had never really gone away, there was a return to the pastoral form once again in the eighteenth to nineteenth centuries as the poets and painters of the Romantic Revival turned to Nature for religious and artistic inspiration. The search for beauty in a wild and isolated landscape, coupled with other bucolic elements that were somehow reassuring and familiar, created their own unique conventions of an Arcadian scene in which the themes of lost innocence, nostalgia and the elegaic were fused together.

The three main sections of a perfect classical, Arcadian scene in a painting usually contain a thin strip of flat foreground within which sheep and shepherds promenade; the odd rock and tree often with a noble edifice[6] in the mid-ground which is preferably reflected in a river, often bridged, or an absolutely calm lake trapped between rockier, mildly cultivated hillocks; and inhospitable crags in the background. Examples still exist of an uncontrived kind: the Vale of Tempe in eastern Greece wedged between Mount Ossa in the south and Mount Olympus in the north; the Lasithi plain in highland Crete; the Bekaa Valley in once peaceful Lebanon. In England, it was extraordinarily original of William Wordsworth to discover Arcadia in the Lake District, although in 1769, the year before Wordsworth's birth, Thomas Gray had searched for and found the 'picturesque' in the wilds of Cumberland.

Ted Hughes, the present Poet Laureate, has suggested that our interest in 'classical' Arcadia or the 'romantic' Picturesque or 'divine' Paradise on Earth, and our urge to visit wild places 'within limits', is mainly because

> they rest us. The thing about these beauty spots, that brings this sense of relaxation and relief, is the state of mind they put us into.

Likening today's tourist who views such 'unadulteration' to a run-down car battery being recharged, he concludes:

> And perhaps this is why we are so pleased to find such places represented in painting or writing – they revive in us these feelings which are as essential to our health as water is to plants.[7]

Although Housman's *A Shropshire Lad* recreates Arcadia in a Shropshire which is only imagined and in many ways hardly pastoral at all in the old sense of the term, there is no doubting the elegiac, nostalgic tone of the work, nor the formidable classical gifts he brought to bear in the cyclic poem in which an uprooted country boy looks back to the innocence and pleasures and, more poignantly, to some frustrations and tragedies of country ways.

In 355 BC Plato imagined a discussion, between Socrates on the one hand and Timaios and Kritias on the other, concerning Atlantis, the long lost city whose inhabitants had put such fear into Athenians over a thousand years earlier. That Atlantis had existed, before it was destroyed by the earthquake which presumably also destroyed the Minoans of Crete, was believed by Plato. That Arkhadia exists is beyond question, and that the pastoral ideal of Arcadia also exists in the imagination is true as long as we wish to remember. But in remembering we are reminded profoundly of our loss – of innocence, of childhood, of the best of ourselves, even as in another sense we regain a wistful kind of innocence as we become aware of our corruption.

It is in this sense that an elegiac tone, springing directly out of the Arcadian tradition, pervades Housman's 'land of lost content'.

NOTES

1. Genesis, ch. 2, v. 8. The Bundahish is similar to Chapter 1 of Genesis.
2. John Milton, *Paradise Lost*, Bk IV, 210–85. Apparently there is still devil worship in inland Portugal, and witches (*bruxas*) and medicine men (*curandeiros*) still cast spells there, as they no doubt always have done.
3. Theocritus, Idyll VII ('Harvest-home'), transl. C. S. Calverley; Bohn's Popular Library Series (G. Bell and Sons, 1913). Robert Wells's recent verse translation is as robust and down-to-earth as Calverley's is lyrical.
4. Kenneth Clark, *Civilization* (BBC and John Murray, 1967).
5. Virgil, *Eclogue* X, transl. C. S. Calverley.
6. The Dissolution of the Monasteries did wonders in supplying artists and poets with splendid crumbling ruins. The Victorians went as far as to knock down part of Ludlow Castle to make it look more 'romantic'.
7. Ted Hughes, *Poetry in the Making* (Faber, 1967).

2 · HOUSMAN'S LIFE AND CAREER

Qui perd une grande foi, a soif de vérité
He who loses a great belief craves the truth
Jean-Jacques Rousseau

VICTORIAN CHILDHOOD: THE PRODIGY

Alfred Edward Housman was born on 26 March 1859, the eldest son of Edward Housman of Bromsgrove, Worcestershire. Housman senior, himself the second son of a family of seven children, enjoyed the comfortable lifestyle of a country solicitor. His own seven children, according to one son, 'worshipped' him. Edward, however, had over the years become a weak, rather wily, though still charming and often eccentric gentleman, and by 1875, when his eldest child was sixteen and his youngest seven, his capabilities, hampered by his addiction to alcohol, had diminished to the point where he could only afford one servant and one horse for the family's use. Years later, in one of his last letters, Alfred wrote: 'My family are tough and long-lived, unless they take to drink.'

Fortunately, Edward's children possessed good brains, received a proper education and were excellently looked after by their mother and, after her death when Alfred was twelve, their stepmother. Both women engendered in Alfred a love for certain poetic passages in the Bible, particularly Ecclesiastes, but the death of his mother affected him profoundly, turning him away from Christianity so that at twenty-one he could declare himself an atheist. Alfred appears to have been a happy though sensitive child, but later, as responsibilities grew, he became increasingly serious and withdrawn.

His mother, Sarah Jane, like his father the child of a vicar and deeply pious, had been a minor champion of the lampoon. Her father, the Reverend John Williams of Woodchester had himself been something of a classical scholar and poet while the Reverend Robert Housman (1759–1838), Housman's father's esteemed father, had earned the title of Evangelist of Lancaster. Maintaining family talents, and enjoying Edward Lear and Lewis Carroll, Housman began in his teens to write good nonsense verse as well as some short serious pieces. Just turned sixteen, he wrote a splendid, somewhat rambling, comic poem to his stepmother (fully quoted in *The Letters of A. E. Housman*). *The Faber Book of Nonsense Verse* (1979) includes eight short poems by Housman which are wise in their wittiness. The following is a good example, written when he was about twenty-eight and still a clerk in the Patent Office, as the last line of this, the first stanza, suggests:

> The shades of night were falling fast,
> And the rain was falling faster,
> When through an Alpine village passed
> An Alpine village pastor:
> A youth who bore mid snow and ice
> A bird that wouldn't chirrup,
> And a banner with the strange device –
> 'Mrs. Winslow's soothing syrup'.[1]

Housman's lifelong interest in the Classics appears to have begun at a very early age. In 1933, when he was seventy-three, he wrote: 'Lemprière's Classical Dictionary which fell into my hands when I was eight, attached my affections to paganism.'[2] The immense size

9

and erudition of this volume gives some indication of his precocity. On his ill-fated twelfth birthday he was given a copy of Shirley Hibberd's *Field Flowers: A Handy Guide for the Rambling Botanist*, and throughout his life his diary entries seldom fail to include a few words about the state of the flora, noted after his daily constitutional ramble. He once told the American author Cyril Clemens that the one book he would take to a desert island would be Alison's *History of Europe*, 'a work I was very fond of as a boy . . . like so many inferior books . . . it had a charm and fascination all of its own'.[3] As another example, A. C. Benson remarked of the middle-aged Housman in his well-known diary:

> I had a long and curious talk with Housman. He spoke of his youthful adoration of Napoleon III, and the Franco-Prussian War was a great shock to him (then aged 11).

Apart from once again highlighting Housman's youthful precocity this also points to another character trait that, having made its first appearance in his youth, was to reappear later in life: a need to hero worship. As he wrote in middle age:

> When I would muse in boyhood
> The wild green woods among,
> And nurse resolves and fancies
> Because the world was young,
> It was not foes to conquer,
> Nor sweethearts to be kind,
> But it was friends to die for
> That I would seek and find.
>
> (LP XXXII)

A letter written to his stepmother when he was approaching sixteen has often been quoted and shows the object of this hero worship taking shape:

> Yesterday I went to the British Museum and spent most of my time among the Greeks and Romans. I looked at your Venus – the Towneley Venus – in the alcove, but I do not admire her. What delighted me most was the Farnese Mercury . . . but I think of all I have seen, what has impressed me most is – the Guards. This may be barbarian, but it is true.[4]

Alfred was educated at the King Edward VI Grammar School, Bromsgrove. He later cited Herodotus as an inspiration to him while he was at school and said that his interest in Classics had been excited by J. E. Bode's *Ballads of Herodotus*.[5] His own schoolboy style as poet was of the Romantic, Swinburnian school, with a syrupy morbidity, though for me the striking qualities of 'The Ruins of Rome' are its simplicity and wistfulness. Already one can smell the aroma of Arcadia. The first stanza runs:

> The city is silent and solemn
> That once was alive and divine;
> And here stands the shaft of a column,
> And there lies the wreck of a shrine;
> But the wild bird still sings in the marshes,
> The wild flower still blooms on the lea,
> And under its infinite arches
> The river runs down to the sea.

At seventeen, Housman received as a gift a book that 'implanted in me a genuine liking for Greek and Latin'.[6] *Sabrinae Corolla* comprised over four hundred

English poems translated mainly into Latin by over ninety old Shrewsbury School scholars. B. H. Kennedy, headmaster at Shrewsbury (1836–66) and a distinguished Latinist, initiated the enterprise and was a leading contributor to the third edition which Housman acquired. When Kennedy left Shrewsbury to become Professor of Greek at Cambridge, a large sum of money was raised, part of which founded the Latin Professorship at Cambridge to which Housman himself was later to be appointed.

The Reverend G. J. Blore, a keen classicist and his first headmaster at Bromsgrove School, was later to reflect that Housman had seemed at school to have a determined, single-minded personality. He had risen to become Head Boy and finished school by winning the major prizes in Greek and Latin verse, as well as prizes for English verse, freehand drawing and French. While at Bromsgrove he won at least thirteen prize books. For his poem 'The Death of Socrates'[7] he was presented with Tennyson's *Poems*, illustrated by Millais; for his poem 'St. Paul on Mars Hill' (unhappily since lost), he won *The Poets of The Nineteenth Century*. These books, and the Bible, were to play an important part in stimulating his imagination and intellect.

Herbert Millington, who took over from Dr Blore while Housman was still at Bromsgrove, took pains to encourage the boy's classical leaning. Later, after Housman failed his Finals at Oxford, Millington offered him a temporary job as Classics teacher and, years after, Housman sent him, on publication, a signed copy of *A Shropshire Lad*. In January 1877, while still seventeen, he failed to win a scholarship to Corpus Christi College, Oxford, but in June he won an open scholarship to St John's, Oxford. He left school a well-educated, confident adolescent, ready to do brilliantly at university; but whereas in his teens Housman had been a prolific writer of verse, in the next decade he wrote scarcely any.

THE YEARS OF PURGATORY: THE SCHOLAR CLERK

'Oxford had not much effect on me, except that I there met my greatest friend.'[8]

To begin with, Housman worked hard at Oxford, studying with Alfred Pollard, a lifelong friend who was later to be Keeper at the British Museum, and great Shakespearian scholar. He was awarded a First Class honours in the interim exams (Honour Moderations), but as he increasingly immersed himself in extracurricular classical studies he began to neglect important areas of the syllabus vital for passing his Finals. Choosing Propertius, and following the example of previous great scholars, he undertook a major task of emendation – to correct and decipher the true meaning of the old text. (His second publication, when he was twenty-nine, was the love poetry of Propertius.) He corresponded with, among others, Hugh Munro, Kennedy Professor of Latin at Cambridge, and became contemptuous of the lax and mediocre teaching of his tutors. He continued, to the point of perversity, to confirm Dr Blore's judgement by being a 'determined personality able to take his own way'.

But distraction – and attraction – came in the guise of another undergraduate at St John's who was a handsome athlete and clever scientist from Kent. When, in their third year, Moses Jackson began to share rooms close to the college with Housman and Pollard, Housman underwent a startling change. To most outsiders and even some close acquaintances Housman appeared aloof, reserved and even frosty, but in the company of Jackson, his spirits were always buoyant.

13

Unwittingly Jackson had deeply inspired Housman. Since Housman needed sad emotions to stir his spirits enough to stimulate his muse he had hardly written any poems at Oxford. However, he did publish his first humorous poem in *Ye Rounde Table*[9] and his first successful serious poem, 'Parta Quies' (MP XLVIII) in another magazine, *Waifs and Strays*. This last poem was the work of an atheist and has been called a 'moving farewell' to his mother; this may be the reason why he never republished it. It moves us because it is constructed with such conviction. It thus ranks among the many good, spirited poems of Housman, although he was only eighteen when he wrote it.

When the results of Finals were announced they proved disastrous. Pollard had gained a First in Greats, Jackson a First in Science, Housman had failed. Six days before sitting the exams his father had suffered a stroke from which he never fully recovered. This certainly did not help his eldest son, who was very fond of his father. There would be a great increase of responsibility at home – but the fact remains that he just had not sufficiently applied himself to the study of the indispensable ancient history and philosophy. Thirty years later, as though by way of a final purge of this galling episode, he was elected an Honorary Fellow of St John's. Significantly, this was the only honour he was to accept out of so many offered him during his long lifetime, including the Order of Merit.

While Jackson and Pollard, having passed the appropriate exams, went on to the Patent Office in London, he on his return home was, as his brother says in *A.E.H.*,

a changed character. It was probably the blow of his failure which caused him to withdraw completely into himself, and become a silent and impenetrable recluse in the midst of his own family.

However, Housman returned to Oxford, gained a Pass, and was soon studying for the Civil Service Examination, which he passed. A highlight of this frustrating eighteen-month period at home, where life was becoming increasingly frugal, was the favourable reception of his first publication. 'Horatiana', about some love poems of Horace, was printed in the *Journal of Philology* in 1882. Eleven years later, in his Introductory Lecture at University College, London, he referred obliquely to how he had felt as a twenty-two year old:

> Man stands today in the position of one who has been reared from his cradle as the child of a noble race and the heir to great possessions, and who finds at his coming of age that he has been deceived alike as to his origin and expectations; that he neither springs of the high lineage he fancied, nor will inherit the vast estate he looked for, but must put off his towering pride, and contract his boundless hopes, and begin the world anew from a lower level.

In one of his last poems there may well be an allusion to May 1881, when his father was ill and examination disaster was imminent:

> On miry meads in winter
> The football sprang and fell;
> May struck the land with wickets:
> For all the eye could tell
> The world went well.
>
> Yet well, God knows, it went not,
> God knows, it went awry;
> For me, one flowery Maytime,
> It went so ill that I
> Designed to die.
>
> (MP XXXIV)

15

Six months after sitting the Civil Service exam he left for London, finding lodgings in Bayswater, and in January 1883 began the tedious but demanding task of checking new claims for trademarks. A few months later he moved to other lodgings in Bayswater, which he shared with Moses and Moses's brother, Adalbert, a classics student at University College. Housman got on well with Adalbert, though it was still to Moses that he directed his secret affection. Even on £100 a year Housman survived, did his duties and paid his rent, but he kept his own family at a distance, writing home infrequently. He learnt to be careful and was not prone to overspending, and he was falling deeply in love – without the object of his devotion having the least suspicion – namely with Moses. Then all abruptly came to an end.

What actually happened we can only surmise, for Housman, now twenty-six, disappeared for a week, much to the Jackson brothers' concern. It is presumed that somehow Housman must have opened his heart to Moses, who possibly was deeply shocked, rejecting the advances of his friend. Ironically the Criminal Law Amendment Act had just been passed which made homosexuality, in any form, illegal. This notorious bill must have made his own predicament all the more alarming to the confused Housman, let alone the shocked Jackson. When he returned Housman moved lodgings and the following year settled more permanently in Highgate. He now had no excuse for neglecting his studies, of Propertius for example, in the British Museum. Self-discipline became routine and he also began to write more poems, though his output was still sparse. The rueful second stanza of XIV of *A Shropshire Lad*, although written six years after he left the Jacksons, indicates his despair at the sudden break:

Ah, past the plunge of plummet,
In seas I cannot sound,
My heart and soul and senses,
World without end, are drowned.

Propertius, the leading elegiac poet in Augustan
Rome, spoke passionately of love and sorrow – which
would therefore have appealed to Housman in any
event. Propertius's writings are also noted for their
obscurity and disorder. When, in 1888, Housman's
Emendationes Propertianae was published, it was so well
received that in 1889 he was invited to join the Cambridge Philological Society by Henry Jackson, a Fellow
of Trinity. He subsequently published a succession of
classical papers, mainly in Latin – all this while still
working full-time at the Patent Office.

Moses and he were friends once again, though not
as close as before. In 1887 Moses had fallen in love with
a young widow, Mrs Rosa Chambers, and decided that
it would be better for him as a husband to pursue an
academic career. He therefore resigned from the Patent
Office, taking up the headmastership of a small school
in Karachi. Housman describes the stoic parting in XXXI
of *More Poems* (the private, posthumous poems it
seems). Written over a year after the event, the almost
casual plainness of speech is interrupted halfway as the
emotion breaks through:

Because I liked you better
Than suits a man to say,
It irked you, and I promised
To throw the thought away.

To put the world between us
We parted, stiff and dry;
'Good-bye', said you, 'forget me.'
'I will, no fear', said I.

> If here, where clover whitens
> The dead man's knoll, you pass,
> And no tall flower to meet you
> Starts in the trefoiled grass,
>
> Halt by the headstone naming
> The heart no longer stirred,
> And say the lad that loved you
> Was one that kept his word.
>
> (MP XXXI)

It is the hesitant, hopeful stanzas after the pivotal 'If' that reveal Housman's need to feel some glimmer of hope in his situation. In the preceding poem, one of futile yearning for Moses Jackson, he had already placed an 'if' by way of enticement. That poem was probably begun just a short time before XXXI, and both poems were started soon after XXXIII of *A Shropshire Lad* which is launched, for once, by another glimmer-of-hope 'if':

> If truth in hearts that perish
> Could move the powers on high,
> I think the love I bear you
> Should make you not to die.

Moses returned almost exactly two years later to marry Mrs Chambers. Housman, kept in the dark, was not invited to the church service in Paddington, and Moses promptly returned to India with his bride. Though no doubt very hurt, it was characteristic of Housman to have sent, belatedly, a message of congratulation.

In 1892 Housman applied and was accepted for the vacant chair of Latin at University College, London. This was an extraordinary feat for a thirty-three year old who had failed his Finals eleven years previously in the very subject he was about to teach. At the same time there was a quickening of pace in his production of poems, so that he wrote more than twenty-five poems in the first half of 1895 alone, nearly all of which were destined for *A Shropshire Lad*. Housman had apparently written to Jackson either in 1896 or 1922, 'You are largely responsible for my writing poetry and you ought to take the consequences.'

THE SCHOLAR AS POET: THE FIRST BOOK OF POEMS

So up and down I sow them
For lads like me to find . . .

ASL LXIII

By the time of *A Shropshire Lad*'s publication in March 1896, Housman was thirty-seven years of age. Thin, medium-sized, dapper, grey-moustached and soft-spoken, he not only inhibited any attempt at familiarity, but could often frighten students and professors alike. His eyes were sharp and when he spoke – which was rarely – it was with 'chiselled speech'. He was beginning to develop the habit of forcibly gesturing with his left hand.

At University College, London he formed a friendship with the Professor of Greek, Arthur Platt, and the Professor of English, the Scotsman W. P. Ker. At lively college Literary Society meetings he lectured on, among others, his favourite, Matthew Arnold, and his fallen idol Algernon Swinburne; he also began jotting down acidic 'one-liners', aimed particularly at erring emendators of classical texts. Later at Cambridge, such comments were to become notorious.

For nearly thirty years from 1903 to 1930 Housman worked on emending the five thick books of Manilius's

Astronomica. Why he should have expended so much of his intellectual energy on such a second-rate Roman poet, incidentally sacrificing a commentary on his beloved Propertius, may puzzle many people. As Housman himself wrote to Robert Bridges, 'I adjure you not to waste your time on Manilius . . . my interest in him is purely technical.'[10] But the 'technical' brilliance of his emendation could lead Professor D. Shackleton Bailey to comment that reading Housman's *Manilius* was 'the most memorable intellectual experience of my life'.

One explanation for this is to be found in Housman's craving for perfection, a 'terror of failure' that intruded equally into the sphere of his personal relationships. 'This is me', he marked by an often-quoted passage in T. E. Lawrence's *The Seven Pillars of Wisdom*, in which Lawrence had painted the following self-portrait:

> There was my craving to be liked – so strong and nervous that never could I open myself friendly to another. The terror of failure in an effort so important made me shrink from trying; besides, there was the standard; for intimacy seemed shameful unless the other could make the perfect reply, in the same language, after the same method, for the same reasons.

Deaths affected Housman acutely, yet he was unable to express emotion 'outwardly'. To assuage his deep grief, for instance, at the death of Adalbert Jackson, who died of typhoid in 1892 aged thirty, and to sing his praise for 'lads that will die in their glory and never be old' (ASL XXIII), Housman wrote in 1893 at least three stirring poems. Two poems, MP XLI and XLII (entitled 'A.J.J.'), were published by Laurence Housman in 1936. The first Boer War (1880–1) also inspired Housman, as it did many other poets, to eulogise over the chance offered to a soldier of achieving

HOUSMAN, AGED 35 AND AT 63, from photographs (*reproduced by courtesy of John Pugh and the Society of Authors*)

VIEW TOWARDS THE CLEE HILLS FROM MT PISGAH, above Fockbury

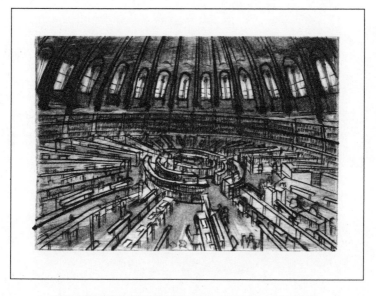

THE READING ROOM IN THE BRITISH MUSEUM

MOSES JACKSON, from a photo (*reproduced by courtesy of the Society of Authors*)

glory and release from a mundane life, or, as in 'The New Mistress' (ASL XXXIV) to forget a failed love affair.

On 27 November 1894 Housman's father had died. I believe that this event enhanced his sense of exile from his native county and its lovely countryside. His Worcestershire childhood and holidays spent at Woodchester on the wooded western edge of the Cotswolds in Gloucestershire had been happy apart from his mother's death. Now he was cut off from his Arcadian dream of childhood, and the resultant nostalgia gave to *A Shropshire Lad* its poignant, wistful flavour:

> Into my heart an air that kills
> From yon far country blows:
> What are those blue remembered hills,
> What spires, what farms are those?

> (ASL XL)

Housman had been thirteen when the family moved from Bromsgrove back to Fockbury. His brothers and sisters nicknamed the top of the hill a few hundred yards from their home, 'Mount Pisgah', because, sitting alone on warm evenings, Alfred had resembled a latter-day Moses scanning the plains of Moab. In fact he was drawing inspiration from the distant sight of the Clee Hills, his 'Promised Land', rising above the wooded middle-ground of the Wyre Forest of western Worcestershire. It may have been this memory and his nostalgia for it, fuelled by his continuing correspondence with the family of Mrs Wise, his godmother, and particularly their German maid and governess Sophie Becker, with whom he kept in touch until the end of her long life, that led him to fix upon Shropshire as the abode of his 'luckless lads'.

While nostalgia was a primal and powerful impulse behind the production of Housman's poetry, anxieties

21

associated with his homosexuality were an important secondary factor. When Oscar Wilde was in Reading Jail Robert Ross had recited passages from *A Shropshire Lad* to him and, when Wilde was eventually released, Housman sent him the book, which was warmly received. To reach and give succour to the suffering homosexual and any lad in despair, as well as to act as a balm to those who had experienced the agony of unrequited love, must have been among Housman's aims:

> – Oh, bring from hill and stream and plain
> Whatever will not flower again,
> To give him comfort . . .
>
> (ASL XLVI)

Soon after his death a newspaper cutting was found by Laurence Housman, pressed alongside a poem in Housman's own copy of *A Shropshire lad*. It concerned a Woolwich naval cadet's suicide in the early summer of 1895 and, poignantly, included part of the cadet's long and detailed suicide note which, thoughtfully, had been left for the benefit of the coroner. The lad had discovered himself to be moved by a stronger desire for men than for women, and had become desperate with feelings of guilt. The poem against which the article had been pressed was this one, written very soon after the tragic event:

> Shot? so quick, so clean an ending?
> Oh that was right, lad, that was brave:
> Yours was not an ill for mending,
> 'Twas best to take it to the grave.

Housman ends prophetically, for we remember the plight of that cadet:

Turn safe to rest, no dreams, no waking;
And here, man, here's the wreath I've made:
'Tis not a gift that's worth the taking,
But wear it and it will not fade.

(ASL XLIV)

While Moses had been near Housman the muse
had been quietened by happiness. Housman was never
a poet of ecstasy, nor of the carefree intimacy that joy
creates, but once Moses had taken his departure – less
dramatic than the cadet's – the muse began to stir:

He would not stay for me; and who can wonder?
He would not stay for me to stand and gaze.
I shook his hand and tore my heart in sunder
And went with half my life about my ways.

(AP VII)

Housman seems to have been writing poems
throughout 1895, although he said it was in the first five
months of the year that he wrote 'in earnest'.[11] The bulk
of *A Shropshire Lad* was written with great speed in a
fervour which he said was almost insupportable. It
seems unlikely that Housman was being misleading, or
simply facetious, in order to divert attention from his
fervent industry, when he continually insisted that *A
Shropshire Lad*'s creation was mainly brought about by
his feeling 'out of sorts'. In January 1895, because he
was suffering from a severe sore throat, he found he
had time to write poetry for much longer than usual.
Coincidentally his emending work had come to a halt
due to the necessity of solving a controversial point in
the text of Propertius. He originally intended to publish
the poems anonymously, which would have released
inhibitions. He later admitted that he craved after fame.

Nearly seventy poems were written in 1895, some of which he never published: fifty for the bulk of *A Shropshire Lad*, with the other thirteen dating as far back as 1890. The Arcadian theme is already present in Housman's original idea of enlisting 'Terence', a rustic character who would tie the poems together in a loose story; was he thereby alluding to Terence, the exiled Greek dramatist, who he knew was brought to Rome as a slave? As we know, the Shropshire Terence – like Housman himself – was removed to London, and thus became an exile from his native land. The scheme was dropped in favour of employing the features of Shropshire's landscape, its towns and villages in the beautiful southern area of the county as delightful backdrops to reminiscences summoned up in the 'cold', anonymous city of London.

Pervaded by an intense melancholia, in which love is rarely requited and always doomed, *A Shropshire Lad* is about friendship sought and, even when apparently sealed, inevitably lost forever; and below this lies the most perplexing eternal question of all – why we exist. Housman's muse may have been gently nurtured by his remarkable feelings for Nature; his love for such an extensive range of poetry may have given him confidence in his own poetical style. Laurence Housman believed his finding the appropriate metre to have released the floodgates of his verse, and his studies of the Classics without doubt helped to canalise that flow into a more disciplined form. What is certain is that he expressed his feelings honestly, lucidly and economically, and favoured a simple, formal metre in poems that belie their occasional troublesome conception.

The poems, originally under the title *The Poems of Terence Hearsay*, were rejected by Macmillan, but just before Christmas 1895 Housman asked his Oxford friend Alfred Pollard to read the manuscript. Pollard

rightly urged Housman to abandon the plan for anonymous publication, and it was he who suggested the
final, immortal title; he then introduced Housman to a
smaller publishing house – who incidentally had first
encouraged Laurence to write – called Kegan Paul,
Trench & Trubner in London's Charing Cross Road. On
the recommendation of their reader, Arthur Waugh
(Evelyn's father), 500 copies of *A Shropshire Lad* were
printed.

A Shropshire Lad was published in Britain in March
1896, 150 copies having been shipped to John Lane in
New York, who published their own edition in 1897.
Though sales were sluggish, reviews on both sides of
the Atlantic ranged from the favourable to the enthusiastic. In September 1898 Grant Richards Ltd published
a further 500 copies and two more editions in 1900
and 1902. By 1906 *A Shropshire Lad* had edged into the
bestseller list of poetry by selling 13,500 copies that
year. At the beginning of the First World War the
pocket edition had become so popular that The Ministry
of War asked Sir Walter Raleigh, the outstanding Professor of English at Oxford, to print some poems from *A
Shropshire Lad* on one of *The Times*'s Broadsheets in
September 1915. Ever since, it has enjoyed universal
appeal. In the 1940s, having been translated into Japanese, a copy was occasionally discovered in the tunic of
a Japanese serviceman; it is said that it was a particular
favourite of Kamikaze pilots. Carl J. Weber has gone so
far as to write that 'by many an American reader *A
Shropshire Lad* has come to be regarded as the most
important book of poetry published in the last
century'.[12]

What is extraordinary is that Housman refused any
royalties from the sales of *A Shropshire Lad*. However, he
wanted as many of the books available at as cheap a
price as possible. It was only after Grant Richards (who

quickly took over the publishing of *A Shropshire Lad* from Kegan Paul) had spent and often squandered money due to his author that Housman insisted, in 1922, that the royalties from sales of *A Shropshire Lad* and *Last Poems* should be paid to him.

A CAMBRIDGE DON: HIS LAST POEMS

Druids and bards (their once loud harps unstrung)
And youths that died to be by poets sung.

Alexander Pope

In January 1911 Housman was appointed Kennedy Professor of Latin at Cambridge, and elected a Fellow of Trinity College. On 9 May 1911 he delivered his Inaugural Lecture, The Confines of Criticism, in which he emphasised that literary criticism should play no part in textual scholarship.

For the next twenty-five years his routine was regular: he lectured once or twice a week to audiences of students, and published a series of brilliant classical papers including the complicated and formidable task of emending Manilius' *Astronomica*. He enjoyed solitary walks after lunch, sometimes two hours long, and enjoyed good food and wine in moderation, especially when dining with The Family, an exclusive twelve-member dining club. He made regular sorties to London to dine with a few male friends, such as his publisher Grant Richards, or William Rothenstein, and then go on to a music hall. When not staying with friends or family in England, he holidayed abroad, preferring to tour France where he could eat well and visit cathedrals. In the 1900s he had a gondolier friend in Venice called Andrea, to whom he paid visits for several years. Strangely, he never actually visited Greece.

It is Housman's last years which are still vivid for one or two people who knew him at Trinity, and I have been told many interesting, authentic little stories about Housman at that time. It is well-known that on his mantelpiece in his study were two photographs: one of Adalbert, young – since he never grew old; the other of his great love, Moses Jackson. While it may be amusing to picture Housman rousing himself from drowsiness in the evening by seizing a pair of dumbells and exercising with them in order to pump the blood faster round his brain, it is sad to think of his gazing at these photographs, which must have brought back vivid memories of the halcyon days of his early twenties.

Tressilian Nicholas, a former Bursar of Trinity who recently died in his 101st year, was kind enough to furnish me with most information from a mind that was clear to the last.

When Mr Nicholas, then only twenty-four years old, was made a Fellow of Trinity in 1912, he found himself in a queue immediately behind his Senior Fellow – by a year – the Kennedy Professor of Latin, in a funeral procession through Trinity College. As they passed under Queen Elizabeth's Gate out of Great Court, Housman remarked to Mr Nicholas: 'I never thought I would pass under this gate in my lifetime.' Like others, Mr Nicholas was amazed that the don was the author of *A Shropshire Lad*: 'I knew Housman many years as a fellow member of the High Table but rarely dared speak to him. He spoke little except to a few close friends and when he did speak he said exactly what he thought, which was apt to be frightening. It seemed to me incredible that so withdrawn and formidable a man could have been the author of *A Shropshire Lad*.'

Mr Nicholas gave me this revealing insight into Housman's character: 'Many of the Fellows were afraid to open a conversation with him in Hall and he once remarked, after listening to some Fellows complaining that another of them was an absolutely insufferable bore, "I liked him – he used to speak to me."' Being a lecturer in Geology it befell Mr Nicholas to be stopped regularly by Housman, who enquired how his godson Gerald Jackson, Moses's eldest son, was progressing as a research student in Geology. But there was also that more familiar, seemingly cold aspect of Housman:

'After the First War a college meeting of all the Fellows of Trinity was held to discuss the erection of a War Memorial to the members of the College who fell in the 1914 War. It had already been decided to engrave their names on the oak panelling in the College Chapel – and very impressive they are, all 660 of them, some of my college friends. A further memorial was under consideration and it was proposed that a swimming pool should be made, and some of the younger Fellows supported this, saying that it would be so useful to the College. This brought Housman to his feet; he said he disapproved of all memorials, but if the College was determined to erect one, he hoped that it would be "totally and utterly useless for any other purpose whatsoever", and sat down. Then he quickly got to his feet again, and said that if the College Council had money to spend on useful purposes, one such purpose would be a flagged path across the cobbled space in front of the Great Gate "to ease the agony of my old bones when I make my daily journey across the cobbles from my rooms in Whewells Court to dine in Hall" (or words to that effect). And before long the Junior Bursar put such a flagged path in hand, which continues to ease the transit across the cobbles, from the Great Gate to Trinity Street. No other memorial was in fact erected.'

If one finds such an attitude distasteful perhaps it should be borne in mind that Housman left memorials, in verse, for many a dead soldier. These are a more fitting and enduring monument than some spiritless exercise in monumental masonry of uniformed soldiery, with less to tell us about the spirit of Man than about the uniform he wore. It was with thoughts of the man as soldier that Housman was preoccupied, not high jinks around a swimming pool. As it turned out, his offhand remark led to an improvement which benefited him particularly.

Concerning Housman's passion for good eating Mr Nicholas is illuminating: 'Housman was critical of the standard of College food and made many entries in the kitchen Suggestion Book. I well remember one which we sometimes turned up to look at in the days of severest food rationing during the Great War: "The salmon today was tasteless, the lamb was both tasteless and tough."

"Look at that," we said, "salmon and lamb on the same day."'

Housman, it must be emphasised, was a gourmet, and whenever in Paris would often make his way to 15 Quai de la Tournelle, where he would join other epicures at the Restaurant de la Tour d'Argent. It was there that, sometime in the 1900s, the famous chef Frederic introduced a fish dish with a sauce mornay to the menu which he christened 'Barbue Housman' – quite a compliment.

At Cambridge it was fortunate that Housman was a Fellow of a college that could afford the very best food. Indeed in all matters of 'domestic' life Housman was cosseted. (When I visited Trinity a few years ago, while the 'bedders' were fearful of losing their jobs, the Dining Hall was luckily still in safe hands.) However, it was churlish of Housman to observe that, having been at Cambridge for twenty years, he had come to realise that it was an asylum in *every* sense of the word. I saw one menu with which Housman entertained about a dozen members of The Family in 1929. Seven bottles of wine, including Cockburn 1878 and Cognac Courvoisier 1869, would do much to repel the onslaughts of madness for many a hard-pressed university dweller who, indeed, had no way of finding immediate solace in families of their own.

Another small but significant recollection by Mr Nicholas confirms Housman's hatred for the sound of church bells, a distaste no doubt dating from his years at Perry Hall, at the very foot of Bromsgrove's imposing church. Referring to Housman's Leslie Stephen lecture in 1933 Mr Nicholas tells me: 'I recall that special measures were taken to silence temporarily the chimes of St Mary's Church during the lecture in case they would put him off.' Had not Housman put ideas into 'the Shropshire lad's' head nearly forty years earlier?

> The bells they sound on Bredon,
> And still the steeples hum.
> 'Come all to church, good people,' –
> Oh, noisy bells, be dumb;
> I hear you, I will come.

>   (ASL XXI)

Just one more first-hand anecdote, albeit rather more gossipy, comes from the late Sir Jasper More, once MP for Ludlow. From over fifty years earlier, he too remembered the show-stopping quality of Housman's clipped small talk which he overheard as he sat near the scholar-poet at High Table in Hall. Some Fellows while dining were discussing the new mode of travel by aeroplane. During the flow of easy conversation about the ability of aeroplanes to carry luggage, a don suggested that aeroplanes could *not* carry luggage. Housman, looking up from his soup, interjected one brief and obviously memorable sentence, 'I happen to know they can', before returning to his soup. Housman was, after all, a pioneer passenger of cross-channel flight. There is no doubt that, to close and trusted friends – and there were few at Cambridge to whom he entrusted his warmth – Housman was unreserved, charming, and talkative. A reading of his hedonistic publisher, Grant Richards' biography, which was concerned with the last half of Housman's life, proves this.[13]

In October 1922 Housman published *Last Poems*. 'About a quarter of this matter belongs to the April of the present year, but most of it dates to between 1895 and 1910,' he ended the short Preface. Indeed numbers III and XXIII were originally destined for inclusion in *A Shropshire Lad*. The disjointed sequence and subject matter in *Last Poems* is not much different from that of *A Shropshire Lad*, both books deriving from a fervent wave of 'personal and lyrical impulse'. Just before the spring of 1922 Housman had heard that Moses was suffering from stomach cancer. In a sudden, astonishing out-pouring, he created or completed fifteen of the forty-one poems in April alone. On publication he posted a copy to Moses, now in hospital, who received it just before dying in January 1923. It was especially for Moses' wedding day, back in 1889, that he had begun 'Epithalamium', and he now hastened to complete it in 1922; it contains this beseeching cry:

> So the groomsman quits your side
> And the bridegroom seeks the bride:
> Friend and comrade yield you o'er
> To her that hardly loves you more.
>
> (LP XXIV)

Nevertheless, in general, Housman's tone has quietened. Though *A Shropshire Lad* was just as hastily

compiled, the lack of firm descriptive background in
Last Poems gives it less homogeneity than *A Shropshire
Lad* which, after all, was originally intended as a series
of ballads centred on a particular young man. I do find
some of the poems particularly beautiful – and number
XL especially so: it exemplifies the slacker pace, with its
more distanced Arcadian allusions, the rise and fall and
considered movement of each sentence and stanza,
compared with the jauntier, spirited gait of earlier
poems. (After a few years of Manilius one might forgive
Housman for slackening his pace; Manilius could be
exhausting.) Christopher Ricks has noted the 'remarkable erotic force of the poem. . . . not that the poem is
erotic and not about nature: it is about both'.[14] It is truly
an elegy set in an arcady with, possibly, a 'trespass' (in
the last stanza) activating the scene. It begins, however:

> Tell me not here, it needs not saying,
> What tune the enchantress plays
> In aftermaths of soft September
> Or under blanching mays,
> For she and I were long acquainted
> And I knew all her ways.
>
> On russet floors, by waters idle,
> The pine lets fall its cone;
> The cuckoo shouts all day at nothing
> In leafy dells alone;
> And traveller's joy beguiles in autumn
> Hearts that have lost their own.

The key is still minor but the tempo less urgent, the
egoism less virile. And you will encounter no dreams of
Elysian fields in the 'hive of hell' ('Hell Gate', LP XXXI,
a minor epic begun in 1905 and completed in April 1922)
or in 'the cave of oracles' (from the war poem, 'The

Oracles', LP XXV). Yeats, sensing the dangers of Housman's maudlin urges, wrote that with Housman 'a mile further and all was marsh'.[15]

In his final public lecture, The Name and Nature of Poetry (1933), Housman, aged 74, said that beginning a poem was for him like a 'morbid secretion . . . like the pearl in the oyster . . . I have seldom written poetry unless I was rather out of health', and described writing it as an 'agitating and exhausting' process. Such statements as 'Poetry is not the thing said but a way of saying it' were enormously provocative to F. R. Leavis whose views were so influential in the English faculty at Cambridge. It was not a search for knowledge as scholarship should be – that, as he had said in 1911, was a meritorious search, but, like primal telepathic vibrations, a means of touching 'something in man which is obscure and latent'. He expressed his feelings through metaphor: the aching sadness of unrequited love; the pathos of criminals who in Housman's eyes were not culpable even when awaiting the hangman's noose.

He had a good stock of morbid ingredients to be excreted from the shell; they were prised out whenever great personal trauma occurred. For example, soon after 1901 when his brother Herbert had died in South Africa, the war poems were 'excreted'; and, as Moses was dying in 1922, in the period of a mere ten days he filled 50 pages of a notebook with poems.

Last Poems contains many soldiering poems though scarcely one was written during the First World War, at which time 8,700,000 lives were lost, over 750,000 of whom were British![16] Yet even during the war and in the early 1920s A Shropshire Lad and Last Poems were immensely popular because they catered for an appetite for nostalgia to which people so readily turn in times of perplexity.

HOUSMAN'S SPIRITUALITY

To see a World in a Grain of Sand,
And a Heaven in a Wild Flower,
Hold Infinity in the palm of your hand,
And Eternity in an hour.

William Blake

Although, like a good 'Romantic', he could focus on wild flowers in particular, 'I took an interest in astronomy almost as early as I can remember', Housman wrote at the age of 73.[17] Quintilian wrote in *c.* AD 50 that no-one could understand poetry unless they had learnt astronomy[18] and, although Housman knew that Christianity had shattered the universal belief in 'divine' constellations, he was a good astronomer. As an aid to emending Manilius, the most famous Roman Stoic astrologer and astronomer, Housman was given an astronomer's globe by his friends the Rothensteins. In July 1926 Francis Dodd, commissioned by St John's College, Oxford, drew an excellent likeness of Housman, with a faint outline of this orb occupying a portion of the background. By that time he was sixty-seven and had completed four of the five volumes of *Astronomica*.

In their two-worlds system the Stoics believed the Earth to be regularly consumed by fire, while the stars remained immutable. This explains their need for stoicism – rather than panic – beneath such an indifferent firmament. To Manilius as to Housman his emendator, even with a gulf of over nineteen centuries between them, the universe seemed equally implacable to humanity. In *A Shropshire Lad* it is enough that 'The gale it plies the sapling double' (XXXI). Apart from the clever use of the nautical term, to 'ply', the word 'gale' is used three times – as if to drum up havoc by repetitive intonation. There is no necessity to involve hurricanes;

it is the steady but unrelenting continuity of adversity that more subtly and realistically shades the beauty of Shropshire with brush strokes of melancholy grey.

The final verse of one of the last poems he wrote (presumably helped by the erotic 'trespass'), is explicit about the casual indifference of the elements:

> For nature, heartless, witless nature,
> Will neither care nor know
> What stranger's feet may find the meadow
> And trespass there and go,
> Nor ask amid the dews of morning
> If they are mine or no.

(LP XL)

This is the very antithesis of the 'primal sympathy' that Wordsworth believed lay deep in human hearts – 'too deep for tears' – as extolled in his 'Intimations of Immortality'. 'Do you really think you can outwit the resourceful malevolence of Nature?' Housman chided a contemporary Classics professor in 1908.[19] For Housman, 'Nature' meant both geographical and atmospheric forms and, of more importance for him as a poet, the human condition. By 'malevolence' he meant the apparent implacable, uncaring harassment that mankind had to endure from 'Nature' in order to become and remain 'comfortable' not only in body but in mind.

To Housman the alleviation of such discomfort was to be found by adopting the attitude of stoicism while, at rare moments, resorting to hedonism as a release. He, like Manilius, thought there was a case for the existence of a supreme controller, in that the heavenly motions were too well regulated to be arbitrary. Sixteen years before he died, when asked by Geoffrey Grant Morrison about his religious opinions, he replied that his mother had the 'High-Church' persuasion and that he himself was a 'High-Church atheist',[20] though his brother Laurence had a niggling suspicion that he believed in the existence of God. And his 'last words', on being told a risqué joke by his doctor, were that he would tell it again when he arrived on 'the Golden Floor'.

Paradoxically at various times in his life he was known to have been interested in the existence of the supernatural or, at least, the unexplained. He was, as mentioned, fascinated by astrology and had his horoscope drawn up by the Cambridge philosopher, Professor C. D. Broad. On one of his first walks in Cambridge through nearby fields he had recognised an avenue of trees: 'Now this *is* strange,' he told his walking companion. 'I have dreamt often of this very place – and now I am here. This is the exact place of my dreams.'[21]

St Mark wrote of Christ's Second Coming, when 'the stars of heaven shall fall, and the powers that are in heaven shall be shaken'.[22] In Revelation, St John the Divine is shown the new twelve foundations of the heavenly city of Jerusalem which had no need of the sun or moon to shine on it: 'for the glory of God did lighten it'.[23] Recalling this, and with perhaps a reference to the hymn 'Abide with Me' where 'earth's vain shadows flee' – and read AP XIV for the 'fleeing of earth's foundations' – Housman wrote 'Epitaph on an Army of Mercenaries':

> These, in the day when heaven was falling,
> The hour when earth's foundations fled,
> Followed their mercenary calling
> And took their wages and are dead.
>
> Their shoulders held the sky suspended;
> They stood, and earth's foundations stay;
> What God abandoned, these defended,
> And saved the sum of things for pay.
>
> (LP XXXVII)

HOUSMAN AT 51, from a photograph taken in 1910 (*reproduced by courtesy of the Mansell Collection, London*)

THE SEED ROLLER, after an etching by C. F. Tunnicliffe

GREAT COURT, TRINITY COLLEGE, CAMBRIDGE

AVENUE OF CHERRY TREES on 'The Backs', towards
Trinity College, Cambridge

With clear allusions to the Old Testament, Housman sorrows for 'The Defeated' at the Last Judgement:

> Amid rejoicing and song
> Remember, my lads, how long,
> How deep the innocent trod
> The grapes of the anger of God.
>
> (AP XIX)

This is reminiscent of 'The Battle Hymn of the Republic', written by Julia Ward Howe in the late nineteenth century:

> Mine eyes have seen the glory of the coming
>   of the Lord,
> He is trampling out the vintage where the
>   grapes of wrath are stored.

Unlike Swift (between whose astrological chart and Housman's there was an uncanny resemblance) the atheist Housman had no fear of dying. He had spent a lifetime voyaging around that topic and needed respite.

In 'Easter Hymn' Housman adopts the use of monosyllabic words to obtain verbal density and emulate the Roman *gravitas*:

> If in that Syrian garden, ages slain,
> You sleep, and know not you are dead in vain,
> Nor even in dreams behold how dark and bright
> Ascends in smoke and fire by day and night
> The hate you died to quench and could but fan,
> Sleep well and see no morning, son of man.
>
> But if, the grave rent and the stone rolled by,
> At the right hand of majesty on high
> You sit, and sitting so remember yet

37

Your tears, your agony and bloody sweat,
Your cross and passion and the life you gave,
Bow hither out of heaven and see and save.

(MP I)

The final line was written at a time of anguish soon after
Housman left his lodgings with the brothers Jackson,
but it was probably not until 1922 that he wrote the rest
of this powerful poem. In that light, the maturing
Housman had accepted the idea of death, although he
still railed against an unjust God who might arbitrarily
decide the fate of 'luckless lads'. 'My chief object in
publishing my verses' he had written, 'was to give
pleasure to a few young men here and there.'[24] Echoing
Propertius's 'A little verse my All that shall remain', this
is the last prophetic quatrain of the final poem in *A
Shropshire Lad* – again written after rejection, this time
by Macmillan:

And fields will yearly bear them
As light-leaved spring comes on,
And luckless lads will wear them
When I am dead and gone.

(ASL LXIII)

If there were no God, no sense of goodness in the
universe, then Housman's memory and poems would
mean little to his 'luckless lads'.

NOTES

1. An untitled poem, of 1887 quoted in Laurence Housman,
   A.E.H. (Cape, 1937). The alliteration 'Mrs. Winslow's
   soothing syrup' owes its existence to the author's dull
   spell in the Patent Office between university and taking

up his first professorship, 1882–92. (Every cloud has a silver lining.)

2. Letter to Maurice Pollet, 5.2.33. MS Lilly Library, Indiana University. First published by Laurence Housman in *A.E.H.* (Cape, 1937). Published by Pollet in *Etudes Anglaises* (1937). Published in *Letters of A. E. Housman*, ed. H. Maas (Rupert Hart Davis, 1971), p. 328.

3. Quoted in Cyril Clemens, *An Evening with A.E. Housman* (1937).

4. Letter, 9.1.1875 MS. University College, London. First published, in the main, in *A.E.H.*

5. Herodotus, born 484 BC and the 'Father of Greek History', wrote in a style that was vivid and poetical but of great clarity. Bode's own style was influenced by Macaulay which must surely have inspired the receptive, romantically minded young Housman.

6. Cambridge Inaugural Lecture, 1911, entitled (by John Carter) The Confines of Criticism (CUP, 1969).

7. The most correct copy is in the Lilly Library, Indiana University.

8. Letter to Pollet, 5.2.33.

9. Housman contributed regularly to *Ye Rounde Table* under the pseudonym 'Tristram'. His nonsense verse was collected and published by Geoffrey Tillotson in 1935.

10. Quoted in *Housman: 1897–1936* by Grant Richards (OUP, 1941), p. 269.

11. Letter to Pollet, 5.2.33.

12. Foreword in the Jubilee edn of ASL, Colby College, Maine.

13. *Housman: 1897–1936.*

14. Christopher Ricks, 'The Nature of Housman's Poetry', in *Essays in Criticism*, XIV (1964).

15. Introduction to *The Oxford Book of Modern Verse* (OUP, 1936).

16. 'Grenadier' (LP V), 'The Oracles' (LP XXV), 'Illic Jacet' (LP IV), 'The Olive' (AP XXIII).

17. Letter to Pollet, 5.2.33.

18. Quintilian, *De Institutione Oratoria*, Bk 1, Ch. IV.

19. Letter to Gilbert Murray, 24.4.1900. M/S Bodleian Library, Oxford. *Letters*, p. 51.

20. Quoted in R. P. Graves' *A. E. Housman: The Scholar-Poet*, p. 187 'High Church atheist' was a phrase remembered by Geoffrey Grant Morris the day after a feast at Corpus Christi, Cambridge (to which Housman was invited) in 1920.
21. Ibid p. 166.
22. Mark, Ch. 13, v. 25.
23. Revelation, Ch. 21, v. 23.
24. Letter to Witter Bynner, 3.6.03. M/S Harvard University. *Letters*, p. 65.

3 · THE CRAFT OF ROMANCE: LOCAL AND LATIN INFLUENCES

Quod spiro et placeo, si placeo, tuum est.
That I express myself and give pleasure (if I give pleasure)
are because of you
Horace, *Ode IV*, iii, 24

For Wordsworth, poetry's appeal lay in 'the small and continual and regular impulses of pleasurable surprise from the metrical arrangement'.[1] For Housman, Wordsworth's poetry contained 'that thrilling utterance which pierces the heart and brings tears to the eyes of thousands who care nothing for his opinions and beliefs'.[2] Housman tenaciously believed that the making and the reading of poetry was an emotional process, while, in contrast, he stipulated what was required of a good emendator:

> To read attentively, think correctly, omit no relevant consideration. . . . and repress self-will . . ., an emendator needs . . . literary perception, congenial intimacy with the author, experience which must have been won by study, and mother wit which must have been brought from his mother's womb.[3]

In 1892, in his Introductory Lecture at University College, Housman advocated the pursuit of knowledge and truth for 'happiness (is) indissolubly bound up with it'. He mentioned, more specifically, that it did not matter if 'the literary faculty of classical scholars is poor and sometimes worse'. In 1911, the thrust of both his Inaugural Lecture at Cambridge (The Confines of Criticism) and the 1921 lecture to the Classical Association (The Application of Thought to Textual Criticism), had been the need for scholars to ignore their 'literary attitudes' and pursue the truth. As both scholar and poet Housman must be credited with practising what he preached. In his last oration, the 1933 Leslie Stephen lecture (The Name and Nature of Poetry), we know he severely provoked F. R. Leavis and the English faculty by insisting that the heart rule the head in a poet. It was in separating emotion from the brain that the spark of controversy was struck. 'Let the scholar amidst the masterpieces of literature maintain the same coolness of head' he had said when comparing classicists to astronomers and botanists in 1911. However, when one turns to his own poetry one finds that 'mother wit' may be much less dominant than the standard of intelligence necessary for such craftsmanship must have been extremely high. While he could say that the intellect of the poet should keep out of poetry, his understanding of poetic forms was keenly developed. He claimed that 'gut reaction' was the seat of his impulse to write poetry, but it was necessary nevertheless for him to attain thorough mastery of the means of arranging strong emotions in their most eloquent form. While W. H. Auden could call Housman's classical work 'dry-as-dust' in a poem called 'A. E. Housman', there is no reason why the imagination and instinct of a poet should not bring life to ancient poetry. No one could deny that seeing the phoenix rise is exciting.

Though he cared little for Dryden or Pope, he frequently resorted for lecture material to the first Augustan Age, during which Horace, Ovid, Tibullus and Virgil claimed their niches in the Temple on Mount Helicon. Lecturing apart, for major emendatory processes, however, he turned to lesser figures such as

Manilius and later poets of 'Silver'. It was mainly Theocritus's powerful bucolic verse that injected vigour back
into country poetry before Virgil's Bucolics and Georgics of the Augustan Age. Using a great variety of
forms, he explored a world of shepherds and herdsmen
– attired in reeking goat skins – who gossiped on their
hillsides and now and again drew on legends involving
lesser Titans such as Heracles's intimate friend Hylas,
or even 'a wayfarer from Crete, young Lycidas'.

The Alexandrian Silver poets, such as Theocritus,
Callimachus, Leonidas of Tarentum and Asclepiades,
classified their poems as, respectively, lyric, elegiac,
brief epic or even briefer epigrammatic. Short volumes
of poems, like Theocritus's *Idylls* or *A Shropshire Lad*,
since they have no narrative thread, are grouped either
by kinship of mood or, for example, by the simple
device of placing a comparatively long poem between
two or more shorter ones. Very few consecutive poems
in *A Shropshire Lad* feature the same metrical character.
Horace was master of this sort of scheme; motifs and
symbols are the key to the organisation of his *Odes*.
Augustan poets ordered their poems not so much by
similarity of subject matter as by means of connection or
contrast between their themes or orchestrated
metaphors. From them, Housman may have learnt
much about how to orchestrate his short poems into
limited sequences.

To see how expertly Housman created atmosphere
with the utmost brevity, one need only read the very
first stanza of the opening poem in *A Shropshire Lad*
which sets us off, this way and that – even to the
heights of God's heaven:

> From Clee to heaven the beacon burns,
> The shires have seen it plain,
> From north and south the sign returns
> And beacons burn again.

A Shropshire Lad contains short poems which explore the full range of melancholia. It is only Housman's practical skill in applying them to different situations that serves to camouflage his desolation. While the Alexandrians and Elizabethans let loose their shepherds and flocks to prance among 'babbling brooks' and pleasant leas where joy prevailed, Housman's golden Arcady, though full of 'hanging woods and hamlets' (ASL XLII) and 'falling stream and standing hill' (ASL XXXVII), is nevertheless badly tarnished by thoughts of death. The Alexandrian Leonidas's themes are similar to Housman's, and in some of Leonidas's poems a voice speaks from the realms of the dead in a manner curiously akin to Housman's plough boy in ASL XXVII – 'Is my team ploughing, . . .'. In the most ebullient Alexandrians there is also a resigned wistfulness and a sympathy for those that bemoan the brevity and the characteristic uneventfulness of human existence. Take this example from Asclepiades, although it tends towards the bliss of young love rather than the pleasant release of death.

> I am not two and twenty,
> And life is a burden to me,
>
> Ye loves why thus maltreat me;
> Why set me afire?

The Greek's lament, that love can be a desolate passion, is worth comparing with the following from *A Shropshire Lad*:

> When I was one-and-twenty
> I heard him say again,
> 'The heart out of the bosom
> Was never given in vain;
> 'Tis paid with sighs a plenty

And sold for endless rue.'
And I am two-and-twenty,
And oh, 'tis true, 'tis true.

(ASL XIII)

For 'shepherd' in Theocritus or Spenser read
'young man', just as Housman's young man is termed a
'lad' some ninety times even in such a small body of
poetry. It is not to the Elizabethans that the defeatism or
the bitterness of Housman's lad are to be attributed,
though they are of course responsible for the earnest
quality of his lyrical and pastoral nostalgia. The main
difference between the two 'lads' is that the Elizabethan, whose eloquence seems indefatigable, would
eventually saunter off whistling after being jilted,
whereas Housman's would come to an untimely and
hapless end. Thus it is not strange that the pastoral
poetry of Sir Philip Sidney, the great and joyous Spenser, or the courtiers who imitated them, found composers eager to set them to music, these melodies subsequently being widely disseminated by players on the
lute and viol.[4] Housman himself was a favourite with
pre-Second World War composers.

Through acquaintance with Shakespeare in his
very lightest moments – he preferred Milton – Housman could (in ASL V) give a sprightly Elizabethan
spring to the step of his 'lad', a step that, for once is
neither halted nor hampered by a slough of despond.
The last lines are no more than a wry aside after some
jolly banter:

– Ah, life, what is it but a flower?
Why must true lovers sigh?
Be kind, have pity, my own, my pretty, –
'Good-bye, young man, good-bye.'

Shakespeare's lad was exceptional; he could suffer

dejection beyond recall if 'slain by a fair cruel maid':

> Not a flower, not a flower sweet,
> On my black coffin let there be strown;
> Not a friend, not a friend greet
> My poor corpse, where my bones shall be
>   thrown.
> A thousand thousand sighs to save,
> Lay me, O! where
> Sad true lover never find my grave,
> To weep there.[5]

In contrast, Housman would have scampered to that grave to strew flowers like confetti! It is for just such sad people that he proffers his 'flower' or 'wreath' even if

> 'Tis not a gift that's worth the taking,
> But wear it and it will not fade.
>
>   (ASL XLIV)

A true act of compassion in Arcadia would be this:

> – Oh, bring from hill and stream and plain
> Whatever will not flower again,
> To give him comfort: he and those
> Shall bide eternal bedfellows
> Where low upon the couch he lies
> Whence he never shall arise.
>
>   (ASL XLVI)

For Housman, though a lover of brightly coloured flowers – the sort with which fresh graves are usually decorated – knows that the dead lad is as dead as flowers which die at every year's end. His lads have no benign female spirit healing their wounds or helping them to win love; they are adept at snatching defeat from the jaws of success. Reading Shakespeare's song in 'Twelfth Night' we suspect that gratification is possible but not necessarily lasting. Ambrosial success may be attained but as easily be destroyed:

> What is love? 'tis not hereafter;
> Present mirth hath present laughter;
> What's to come is still unsure:
> In delay there lies no plenty;
> Then come kiss me, sweet-and-twenty,
> Youth's a stuff will not endure.[6]

Depending on how it is construed, it may seem that another of Shakespeare's lads plays it with passion, though not without guile:

> Doubt thou the stars are fire;
> Doubt that the sun doth move;
> Doubt truth to be a liar;
> But never doubt I love.[7]

Housman was twenty-six when he suffered what must have been the cataclysmic rejection of his love for Moses Jackson. In his self-pity the 'lad' too is wounded in love and rues the day he bothered with girls. With the plaintive sigh of wisdom through hindsight, he counsels in the course of the poem that so resembles Ascelepiades':

> When I was one-and-twenty
> I heard a wise man say,
> 'Give crowns and pounds and guineas
> But not your heart away . . .'

> > (ASL XIII)

Can it be best for heroic lovers that they die young?

In *A Shropshire Lad* three courses are open for the defeated lover: to commit suicide, to join the army, or to live his days out in a kind of bitter defiance. Housman, like the Ancients, used the epithet 'golden' to describe such heroism. 'You are a dear, Phaedrus, and golden indeed,' Socrates says in Plato's *Phaedrus*. The Latins too were fond of it: 'Qui nunc te fruitur credulus aurea', Horace wrote, and Shakespeare frequently employed the adjective:

> Golden lads and girls all must,
> As chimney sweepers, come to dust.[8]

Housman had 'golden friends' who, like 'golden calves', he might adore, but they were reduced to mortality, and, had it not been for the poet's power to immortalise, would have been completely forgotten:

> Let me mind the house of dust
> Where my sojourn shall be long.
>
> (ASL XII)

Moreover, 'still, I think in newer veins/Frets the change-less blood of man' (ASL LV). For the lamenting lad was in love with the grave, a comfortable, external, even 'corrupting grave' (AP XXIII), where Housman hoped he would meet up again with Moses Jackson, his golden friend. Housman's graves are a veritable charnel house and if his Athlete, who in *A Shropshire Lad* dies young, returns to haunt the scene of his victory, then it is not just his bones that are the 'Immortal Part' (ASL XLIII). The poet himself has redeemed the victor by singing his praises. Just as Alcestes won his garlands of green bay from Aeneas in the archery contest,[9] so Housman's lad has the victor's garland, 'briefer than a girl's', for ghosts

to admire (ASL XIX). Rarely touching upon their girls,
Housman sang of 'luckless lads' and 'honest fellows', of
real though exceptional young men, every one all too
mortal. As Theocritus put it at the start of Idyll XVI
translated by Calverley:

> What fires the Muse's, what the minstrel's lays?
> Hers some immortal's, ours some hero's praise,
> Heaven is her theme, as heavenly was her birth:
> We of earth earthy, sing the sons of earth.

Housman's 'rose-lipt' maidens and lightfoot lads know
a bit about love:

> If at death's own door he lies,
> Maiden, you can heal his ail.
>
> (ASL VI)

He enjoyed visiting music-halls and would have been
familiar with the song 'Barbara Allen':

> All in the merry month of May
> When green buds they were swelling,
> Young Jemmy Grove on his deathbed lay
> For love of Barbara Allen.

Once smitten, there is no turning back for lads like
Master Grove:

> His folly has no fellow
> Beneath the blue of day
> That gives to man or woman
> His heart and soul away.
>
> (ASL XIV)

But there may be one more glimmer of hope:

If truth in hearts that perish
Could move the powers on high,
I think the love I bear you
Should make you not to die.

(ASL XXXIII)

Poems VI and XII are the ones that express most about
the dangers of falling in love; the poet here speaks
feelingly:

Lovers' ills are all to buy:
The wan look, the hollow tone . . .

(ASL VI)

and so on. In *A Shropshire Lad* love is always a danger-
ous emotion, but at least such steady attributes as
honesty and integrity struggle manfully through. Of the
lad's 'hand' Housman has no doubts:

So many an honest fellow's fist
Had well-nigh wrung it from the wrist.

(ASL XXXVII)

A few lines later, with fighting words, the value of
integrity is extolled:

Be clean then; rot before you do
A thing they'd not believe of you.

The final word of that poem is 'grave', although as
usual it has begun cheerfully enough and bounds forward until it reaches this inevitable end.

While the industries of Victorian England flourished,
so too did a need to find solace in a countryside being

50

steadily depopulated. Theocritus would have condoned Wordsworth's choice as setting for his poems of

> low and rustic life . . . because in that situation the essential passions from the heart find better soil in which they can attain their maturity, are less under restraint and speak a plainer and more emphatic language . . . and lastly because in that situation the passions of men are incorporated with the beautiful and permanent forces of nature.[10]

Evelyn Waugh satirised the Arcadian myth of rustic life in *Scoop* (1938) in which Mr Salter tentatively suggests to Boot, 'I say, how about some zider?' Two thousand years earlier Theocritus encapsulated this difference in 'Town and Country' (Idyll XX), and Housman alludes to the sullen reception that country lads can encounter in large towns in ASL LI, LII and the following:

> . . . I see
> In many an eye that measures me
> The mortal sickness of a mind
> Too unhappy to be kind.
>
> (ASL XLI)

Housman's lad was cast in the mould of an upright, bold, athletic young countryman, but not too old to be a 'lad'. Two things contributed to the lad's loss of Arcady: his manifest need to experience anxiety about his sad quest to ascertain the purpose of life; and in consequence, his embittered wooing of death. As time wore on Terence, Maurice, Ned or Dick[11] became concerned less with the beauties of the countryside than with the loss of friends. Exile heightens nostalgia. Housman must have had in mind Blake's poem 'London' when he wrote the London poems in *A Shropshire Lad*.[12] There are similarities between Housman's Shropshire Lad and Blake's Londoner who, a few generations older, experienced the same sort of reactions as Housman's as he dolefully walked the streets:

> I wander through each chartered street,
> Near where the chartered Thames does flow,
> And mark in every face I meet
> Marks of weakness, marks of woe.

Arnold, in *The Scholar Gipsy*, had written that life seemed no longer to run 'gaily as the sparkling Thames'. Had the Shropshire lad adhered to the Theocritan regions of almost unthinking joy, where Pan unceasingly played his pipes, one would have tired of Shropshire's spring-green meadows and 'blue remembered hills'. Like Keats, Housman drew on his wider imagination, stimulated by indignation at the homosexual's and soldier's unfortunate lots, and lent depth by profound reflections on unrequited love and the loss of Arcady. Between 1896 and 1922 thoughts of Arcady slowly faded until it became 'long since forgotten'. The sadness that beset the Shropshire lad and which had, like the Erymanthean Boar, roamed the hills, was now turned inwards until it was preoccupied only with itself. The mental, emotional and spiritual struggle no longer dictated a bodily presence in the hills and valleys. Indeed, in *Last Poems* there is hardly a glimpse of Shropshire; it is the theme of sorrow that groups the poems together, in a way that at first sight might appear arbitrary.

Housman's earliest poetic influence came from sentimental romantic verse, such as those by G. A. Simcox (1841–1905) which did much to inspire his drama 'Hell Gate' (LP XXXI); as a youngster, though unable to fend off Swinburne, he was also strongly drawn to Milton and Arnold. He absorbed the Romantics, admiring Byron, Keats and Shelley. Notebooks from his early

HOMER AND AESCHYLUS

LANDSCAPE, after the wash drawing by Claude Lorrain (*reproduced by kind permission of the Lobo Trust*)

VALLEY OF VISION, from the wash drawing by Samuel Palmer

HOUSMAN AGED 67, from the drawing by Francis Dodd, 1926 (*reproduced by kind permission of the National Portrait Gallery, London*)

teens contain copies of sentimental, third-rate poems on the subjects of death, separation and grief. In 1928 he wrote that 'the influence of Heine is evident in *A Shropshire Lad*. For Keats I have the greatest admiration, but I should not have thought that my writing had any affinity to his'[13]; and in 1933 he commented of *A Shropshire Lad*, 'Its chief sources of which I am conscious are Shakespeare's songs, the Scottish Border ballads and Heine.'[14] Of Heinrich Heine (1799–1856), Arnold wrote:

> The magic of Heine's poetical form is incomparable; he employs this form with the most exquisite lightness and ease, and yet it has at the same time the inborn fulness, pathos, and old-world charm of all true forms of popular poetry.[15]

Here is Heine's 'Ad Finem', translated by Elizabeth Barrett Browning:

> The years they come and go,
> The races drop in the grave,
> Yet never the love doth so
> Which here in my heart I have.
>
> Could I see thee but once, one day,
> And sink down so on my knee
> And die in they sight while I say,
> 'Lady I love but thee!'[16]

In many ways Housman's poetry was similar to that of Thomas Gray's, though his poetic diction displays less than Gray's ability for elaboration of structure. But although Housman insisted that, for him, writing poetry resulted chiefly from a gut reaction, the more one studies his prosody the more one is impressed by his superb craftsmanship and by such variety of form in so few poems. What is remarkable is his economy of syllables – which I shall shortly illustrate – an economy as rigorous as that exhibited by Heine in the poem above. Indeed there is not a single instance of a five-syllable word in the whole of *A Shropshire Lad*. Besides a mere seven of four syllables there are just over fifty of three; all the remainder of its vocabulary consists of dissyllables and monosyllables. This must have been the Latin influence at work, an inflected language in which much meaning may be concentrated into a single word – which makes for brevity. In 1903, Housman nonchalantly wrote: 'I suppose that my classical training has been of some use to me in furnishing good models, and making me fastidious, and telling me what to leave out.'[17] It also taught him such mannerisms as this sort of play on words so characteristic of Ovid:

> And set you at your threshold down,
> Townsman of a stiller town.
>
> (ASL XIX)

or this

> The goal stands up, the keeper
> Stands up to keep the goal.
>
> (ASL XXVII)

In his use of words, he imposed upon English not only these monosyllables – a pleasing mannerism – but an equally pleasing taste for the deliberate archaism so often used by poets of that *fin-de-siècle* period.

It is fascinating to see how Housman, so particularly a lyric poet, not only shows his ability in mixing his rhythms from poem to poem, but uses such a wide range of forms. He juxtaposes iambics and trochaics from line to line – often within the line itself – and from stanza to stanza, in the course of one poem. He first tightens, then loosens, his instinctive hold on the straightforwardly constructed ballad by introducing hints of the epic, the elegy or the ode. In 1922 he wrote: '15 [of LP] is not much in itself, and I only put it in for variety, as I did no. XX in *A Shropshire Lad*'[18]. With Housman message and mood took priority, means being secondary, and yet in even the simplest looking quatrain there is to be found subtlety and a conscious purpose to make the poem effective. In ASL LIV the feminine endings of the first and third lines in both stanzas prolong the sad lilt which is all the more sad for being cut short by the hard, curt words that end the alternate lines:

> With rue my heart is laden
> For golden friends I had,
> For many a rose-lipt maiden
> And many a lightfoot lad.
>
> By brooks too broad for leaping
> The lightfoot boys are laid;
> The rose-lipt girls are sleeping
> In fields where roses fade.

The boys are too young and spindly for their feet to span country streams, while the girls smell of hay and roses. The contrasts in rhythm help to bring out the difference between boys and girls.

Laurence Housman, annotating his brother's four Notebooks, wrote 'rough, draft, many corrections' by the first line of ASL XLVIII which lies between poems he dates 1891–2 and February 1893. The second draft, again undated, is found two headings below a poem written in the Notebooks in August 1893. As his poetry was provoked by sad events it is unlikely to have been a

55

creation from the happy time of his appointment as
Professor of Latin in London in June 1892, but rather
five months later, when Adalbert Jackson was struck
down by typhoid. It is a powerful poem which, as
Laurence thought of all his brother's poems, was all the
better for much correction and rethinking:

> Be still, my soul, be still;
> > the arms you bear are brittle,
> Earth and high heaven are fixt
> > of old and founded strong.
> Think rather, – call to thought,
> > if now you grieve a little,
> The days when we had rest,
> > O soul, for they were long.
>
> Man loved unkindness then,
> > but lightless in the quarry
> I slept and saw not; tears fell down,
> > I did not mourn;
> Sweat ran and blood sprang out
> > and I was never sorry:
> Then it was well with me,
> > in days ere I was born.
>
> Now, and I muse for why
> > and never find the reason,
> I pace the earth, and drink the air,
> > and feel the sun.
> Be still, be still, my soul;
> > it is but for a season:
> Let us endure an hour
> > and see injustice done.
>
> Ay, look: high heaven and earth
> > ail from the prime foundation;
> All thoughts to rive the heart are here,
> > and all are vain:

> Horror and scorn and hate
> and fear and indignation –
> Oh why did I awake?
> when shall I sleep again?
>
> (ASL XLVIII)

A close similarity of rhythm continues throughout the poem between the equivalent lines of each stanza. I shall look particularly at the first stanza which, to me, reads exactly like a psalm, the caesura reinforcing this impression. With its *gravitas* it reads like a portentous speech. The punctuation creates feelings of ponderous movement, which is unrelenting. Indeed each stanza is a complete statement. It starts, like Gray's *Elegy*, with a flowing rhythm, with a hissing, grandiose sound. One senses that the words 'the arms you bear are brittle' refer to the soul's being like an untrustworthy ogre that might snap bones like twigs were it not careful. 'Brittle', with its feminine ending, echoes the 'ill' sound of 'still' at the start, while in the last stanza, 'foundation' fades away, as does 'indignation' – long words that emphasise the simplicity of the intervening monosyllables. While there is much mixing of vowel sounds in the whole poem, almost all the vowels are let loose in the first line of the last stanza: 'Ay, look: high heaven and earth ail from the prime foundation'. Housman's use of the archaic 'ail' – here, as earlier in 'maiden, you can heal his ail' – is a characteristic Housman touch. In the third line of the third verse the intonation is repeated. In Psalm 119, in the King James Bible, the same kind of implacable repetition, akin to a musical ostinato, is to be found:

> My soul cleaveth unto dust: quicken thou me according to thy word. (v. 25)
> My soul melteth for heaviness: strengthen thou me according unto thy word. (v. 28)

This construction, of following opening statement with the voicing of personal feelings is, for lyric poetry, highly organised.

In the second line of the first stanza Housman opens with trochee, then, with an alliterative spondee *en route*, he ends on an iambic run of 'O' sounds. The next line starts with another spondee, then pauses briefly before settling into iambics throughout the last line. The other stanzas all begin forcefully, especially the last, its emphatic spondees being followed by gentle iambics. The variety of rhythms that Housman uses are invariably for specific purposes and in these instances he wants strong emphasis, equally placed. The rhyming is simple: *a b a b*, sometimes in ballads and still in use. The metre consists of the hexameters commonly found in elegiac verse. Variety derives from the initial impact of spondees. The remaining three stanzas have feminine endings in their first and third lines; these lines in the second stanza begin with spondees – a favourite foot in Latin poetry though rare in English verse which may therefore have had special appeal for Housman.

Let us now take three consecutive poems from *A Shropshire Lad*, begun in May, January and April 1895 respectively; we shall begin with the middle one, 'The Welsh Marches'.

> High the vanes of Shrewsbury gleam
> Islanded in Severn stream;
> The bridges from the steepled crest
> Cross the water east and west.
>
> The flag of morn in conqueror's state
> Enters at the English gate:
> The vanquished eve, as night prevails,
> Bleeds upon the road to Wales.

Ages since the vanquished bled
Round my mother's marriage-bed;
There the ravens feasted far
About the open house of war:

When Severn down to Buildwas ran
Coloured with the death of man,
Couched upon her brother's grave
The Saxon got me on the slave.

The sound of fight is silent long
That began the ancient wrong;
Long the voice of tears is still
That wept of old the endless ill.

In my heart it has not died,
The war that sleeps on Severn side;
They cease not fighting, east and west,
On the marches of my breast.

Here the truceless armies yet
Trample, rolled in blood and sweat;
They kill and kill and never die;
And I think that each is I.

None will part us, none undo
The knot that makes one flesh of two,
Sick with hatred, sick with pain,
Strangling – When shall we be slain?

When shall I be dead and rid
Of the wrong my father did?
How long, how long, till spade and hearse
Put to sleep my mother's curse?

(ASL XXVIII)

Metrical variety is much less evident in these tetra-
meters, although the first and second stanzas feature
dactyls and inversions, trochees and iambics side by
side Again, though less probably, it might be said that
'High' in the first line is left out on a limb, while 'the
vanes' lead off the iambics, but one ought to start by
inspecting the first word, rather than paying particular
attention to the last. There is a plethora of sibilants in
the first stanza, and the alliterative 'Severn stream'
warns us that Housman is going to concentrate his
efforts upon this element of sound, as indeed he pro-
ceeds to do throughout the remaining stanzas. For
instance, these lines, beginning with emphatic hissing
trochaics, show Housman's adept mastery behind the
flow of such lines as

> Sick with hatred, sick with pain,
> Strangling – When shall we be slain?

What is so effective here is how much is said in so few
words. The first six stanzas, in turn, set the scene, paint
the historical background, and provide a commentary
on its relevance from a personal point of view. This is a
great achievement.

The poem following, 'The Lent Lily', is not in a
common form for Victorian poetry, but Housman's plan
here is a simple *a b a b b*; note how he starts the first
verse boldly, a stratagem shown to its best advantage in
'Wake: the silver dusk returning' ('Reveille', IV) and
'Shot? so quick, so clean an ending?' (XLIV). Apart from
the initial, arresting caesura, the punctuation implies no
more than a brief pause at the end of each second line.
In the opening stanza the penultimate line, with the
melancholy tone of its 'hollow', exemplifies Housman's
perceptive imagination – his 'mother's wit':

'Tis spring; come out to ramble
The hilly brakes around,
For under thorn and bramble
About the hollow ground
The primroses are found.

And there's the windflower chilly
With all the winds at play,
And there's the Lenten lily
That has not long to stay
And dies on Easter day.

And since till girls go maying
You find the primrose still,
And find the windflower playing
With every wind at will,
But not the daffodil,

Bring baskets now, and sally
Upon the spring's array,
And bear from hill and valley
The daffodil away
That dies on Easter day

(ASL XXIX)

The point of the poem is effectively emphasised by the little stinging inversion of sentiment – death and joy – in the very last line.

The poem preceding 'The Welsh Marches' has, as is often the case in Housman, no title. It is an example of what is known as the Dramatic Ballad, incorporating a dialogue. As Browning is famed for his dramatic monologue, so Housman, perhaps through Vaughan Williams' and Britten's settings, is widely and rightly famed for this poem; in addition it was Hardy's favourite.

'Is my team ploughing,
That I was used to drive
And hear the harness jingle
When I was man alive?'

Ay, the horses trample,
The harness jingles now;
No change though you lie under
The land you used to plough.

'Is football playing
Along the river shore,
With lads to chase the leather,
Now I stand up no more?'

Ay, the ball is flying
The lads play heart and soul;
The goal stands up, the keeper
Stands up to keep the goal.

'Is my girl happy,
That I thought hard to leave,
And has she tired of weeping
As she lies down at eve?'

Ay, she lies down lightly,
She lies not down to weep:
Your girl is well contented.
Be still, my lad, and sleep.

'Is my friend hearty,
Now I am thin and pine,
And has he found to sleep in
A better bed than mine?'

Yes, lad, I lie easy,
I lie as lads would choose;
I cheer a dead man's sweetheart,
Never ask me whose.

(ASL XXVII)

The use of dactyls makes it easier to distinguish the two voices, the one living, the other dead. The start of each of the ghost's four questions, as in the third verse: 'Is football playing . . .', could conceivably be construed as a metre termed 'tribach' – three equal accents on 'Is football' before the trochee 'playing'. The ghost is in for a rude awakening at the very moment that the bilateral banter comes to an end. The inversion, the counter-point, here is played out by the characters themselves. 'The Deserter' (LP XIII) is the only other true dialogue by Housman, and is revealing of his usual views on the unfairness when love and war combine.

In ASL XXVI there are two ten-line stanzas of couplets; Keats used ten lines in several odes. But not only does it regularly switch metre, rhythm and length, it acquires new dimensions through this increase from one to two people speaking in the poem. Talking in whispers an aspen tree, seeing all, is musing morosely but prophetically. Here is Arcadia person-ified. Housman often introduces a hidden voice to add realism to a poem – realism which the anguish of the elusive Terence Hearsay imported into *A Shropshire Lad*. The whole of VIII, with its cold dinner, is a dramatic monologue purportedly by the murderous hero. LXII – 'Terence, this is stupid stuff . . .' – introduces a sense of theatre, some amiable 'crack' being followed by philo-sophical asides. There is no doubt that, like the Ancient Mariner, the lad is now 'a sadder and a wiser man'. In XXXIV, the word 'sick' is again favoured: 'Oh, sick I am to see you, will you never let me be?' The lad parries the angry thrust of dismissal with a practical riposte: he 'joins up'. The lad is not totally discomfited if trees address him or if bones speak up, as in XLIII; nor do we, the readers, feel it at all odd. Among the achieve-ment of such poems is our willing and total suspension of disbelief. A quasi-apostrophe is used in the repetitive questioning of 'Lancer': 'Oh, who would not sleep with the brave?' (LP VI), while a true apostrophe is to be found at the end of LP XXV. This poem, with its common-hymn measure of eight-foot iambics interspersed with ones of seven-feet, is crowned by the last reflective, majestic stanza. The oracle speaks. There will be no new Thermopylae. As the Sirens once sang on their fabled island, so in Housman's Arcady alluring voices are heard from all around us and bewitch us.

The first stanza in ASL XXXVI shows Housman's careful use of repetition and alliteration:

> White in the moon the long road lies,
> The moon stands blank above;
> White in the moon the long road lies
> That leads me from my love.

The evocation of mood seems effortless,[19] but again note every word except 'above' is a monosyllable. Rhythm is stifled by the baldness of the four statements. The world is blank white, the tone deadpan. When the trudging begins, the syllables expand, although there is no law of expanding syllables which states that polysyllables establish the more 'mood' the longer they become:

> Still hangs the hedge without a gust,
> Still, still the shadows stay:
> My feet upon the moonlit dust
> Pursue the ceaseless way.
>
> The world is round, so travellers tell,
> And straight though reach the track;
> Trudge on, trudge on, 'twill all be well,
> The way will guide one back.

> But ere the circle homeward hies
> Far, far must it remove:
> White in the moon the long road lies
> That leads me from my love
>
> (ASL XXXVI)

The journey is going to be a tedious round and ploughing, too, is a tedious process, as described in ASL VII: 'When smoke stood up from Ludlow', where the repetition of the first line of the third stanza, 'Lie down, lie down, young yeoman', in the first line of the last, is used for exactly the same reasons:

> 'Lie down, lie down, young yeoman;
> The sun moves always west;
> The road one treads to labour
> Will lead one home to rest,
> And that will be the best.'

The last line here is an instance of Housman's creative use of bathos. Words that further emphasise the patient drudgery in ASL XXXVI are 'ceaseless' (stanza 2), 'round' (st. 3), and 'circle' (st. 4). As the Earth rotates so our lives begin and end, bringing us full circle. Housman is not delivering an oration on the value of knowledge. He advocates the merit of trudging the long 'circular' road of life but not in any particular pursuit of wisdom, satisfaction and goodness – ideas he discussed in his Introductory Lecture of 1892.

In the poem the 'trudger' has just left his lover for good. Those who have lost or been separated from their loved one will know that when the light goes out of their life, they must nevertheless pick themselves up and carry on. They tell us: 'Life must go on'. This is what this poem encapsulates: the repetition of sounds, and of whole phrases, emphasises the emotion. In the early 1900s Housman wrote a string of richly romantic poems that hang on the east-west divide between himself and Moses Jackson. Moses was to spend another ten years or so in India before, in 1911, emigrating to Canada, yet it was before this that Housman wrote 'Comrade, look not on the west', repeated three times in the forty-four lines of 'The West' (LP I), while 'The rainy Pleiads wester' (MP XI) is repeated twice in eight lines. About this time, he also began, in 1902, 'The Land of Biscay' (MP XLVI) where 'Down the waterway of sunset drove to shore a ship of gold'. Housman sent that ship away; had it been brought safely to harbour, thus allaying the spirit of yearning, the poetry that this fuelled would have dried up.

A pertinent little ditty, progeny of the humour of his childhood, with a great deal to say about how a lad, or even a lass, feels when love has died is this:

> Oh, when I was in love with you,
> Then I was clean and brave,
> And miles around the wonder grew
> How well did I behave.
>
> And now the fancy passes by,
> And nothing will remain,
> And miles around they'll say that I
> Am quite myself again.
>
> (ASL XVIII)

It is difficult to walk the tightrope of such simplicity without tumbling into the net of clumsiness: it has to be admitted that Housman takes one or two tumbles in the cause of colloquialism.

Housman was master of the epigrammatic, dramatic 'entrance' and 'exit' lines: 'Shot? so quick, so clean an ending' is a mode of dramatic opening; an example of a wistful ending, again from *A Shropshire Lad*, is 'Mithridates, he died old' (echoing the cryptic epigraph prefacing Conrad's *Heart of Darkness*, 'Mr. Kurtz, he dead'). These controlled convolutions of rising and falling metre, and of stanza formation, in a strange way remind me of how Housman, when still a boy, succinctly explained the motion of Earth and Moon around the Sun to his brother and sister at home on the lawn at Bromsgrove – a story related by Laurence in *A.E.H.* But, to return to Housman's pertinence as a poet, if he has a pleasant vice, it is to veer suddenly into the ditch of the banal, lest we should lose sight of reality. He understates well in this next 'conversation piece', but his aim here, of being laconic, compares ill with Rupert Brookes' 'honey still for tea':

> 'Long for me the rick will wait,
> And long will wait the fold,
> And long will stand the empty plate,
> And dinner will be cold.'

> (ASL VIII)

Not only does 'long' become monotonous in repetition – and the punctuation is surely intentionally basic – but the last line has a raw quality that is inelegant. Housman was also dealing, here, with a drastic domestic upset: murder had been committed on the home farm. But the chores around the farm have to be done, come what may – and meals cooked, day in, day out, year in, year out.

Housman liked the macabre humour of limericks, as shown by his humorous verse, and he was fond of fashioning down-to-earth practical statements for serious effect. There are poems where Housman speaks to the 'inner man' – in his term, soul 'vibrating' to soul – but he could vary the mood, like a change of key or tempo in music, with great skill. Such down-to-earth intrusions as that 'cold dinner' could be interpreted as a 'dig' at the sickly-sweet desserts dished up by Rossetti and Swinburne.

Certainly Housman could be subtle in his irony, as in '1887' (ASL I), the year of Victoria's Golden Jubilee. Here the opening lines of the National Anthem, 'God save our gracious Queen', are ritually run through the tenses, to make one wonder whether God's undue concern with the head of state might not be somewhat myopic. For if her soldiers fight hard, the Queen will be saved: 'Oh God will save her, fear you not'; especially if soldiers like those of the 'Fifty-third' beget similar warrior sons. Although there was no danger of Housman advocating pacifism, he, like many others, may have become a little jaded with the Old Queen. There is further irony in his fleeting reference to the Crucifixion in the fourth stanza:

> To skies that knit their heartstrings right,
> To fields that bred them brave,
> The saviours come not home to-night:
> Themselves they could not save.

Thus is the fallibility of both God and State impertinently hinted at in the opening poem of the book. But no one, however anarchic, would feel proud of having penned the dénouement of ASL XXXIV:

> 'I will go where I am wanted, where there's
>   room for one or two,
> And the men are none too many
>   for the work there is to do;
> Where the standing line wears thinner
>   and the dropping dead lie thick;
> And the enemies of England
>   they shall see me and be sick.'[20]

IN THE WELSH MARCHES

VENICE, after 'L'isola San Giorgio' by Guardi

OLIVES

THE SEVERN AT BUILDWAS

Quite different is Nature's 'overcoat' from a poem written in the prolific spring of 1922. Here is the better second and final stanza with its emphatic start, so akin to Tennyson's 'Break, Break, Break', or Housman's own 'Be still, my soul, be still':

> Fall, winter, fall; for he,
> Prompt hand and headpiece clever,
> Has woven a winter robe,
> And made of earth and sea
> His overcoat for ever,
> And wears the turning globe.
>
> (LP XX)

Wordsworth has Lucy 'Rolled round in earth's diurnal course, / With rocks, and stones, and trees', but did Housman, from *A Midsummer Night's Dream*, also bear away 'We the globe can compass soon' to his bleak midwinter lair?[21]

Of all sixty-three poems in *A Shropshire Lad* only two are immediately followed by another sharing identical metre, rhythm and rhyming scheme.[22] Taking four poems, three from *Last Poems* and one from *A Shropshire Lad*, Housman, who is not over-fond of the five-line poem, varies each so well that, even though the rhyming schemes follow previous patterns, their metrical rhythms are different. 'Bredon Hill' (ASL XXI) goes *a b c b b*; LP XVIII and XXXVIII are *a b c c b*, while LP XXXIX adopts the 'Bredon' system. Housman is quite capable of stirring into the mixture the glories of heady, swinging, Swinburnian anapaests – as in ASL XXIII, or Kiplingesque rhythms – as in ASL XXXIV, trochaic tetrameter catalectics – as in 'Terence, this is stupid stuff' (ASL LXII), and most of LV; and there are even to be found trochaic dimeter catalectics with double anacrusis. But, for all these differing techniques, Housman insisted that poetry was a natural effusion for him. Only rarely are we treated to an insight into the hard labour behind his muse:

> 25 [of LP] dissatisfies me too, but not quite in the same way. The first and last stanzas came into my head; the middle ones are composed.[23]

Laurence wrote in his biography that he was sure his brother had torn out of his Notebook the page that would have clarified the order in which the stanzas of the last poem of *A Shropshire Lad* were composed. It was a riddle posed by Housman himself when he asked, in the course of the 1933 lecture, if anyone could guess the order in which these stanzas had been written.

I came across a splendidly detailed Japanese edition of *A Shropshire Lad*, with translations and copious commentary.[24] In this book a magnificent obsession with derivations had led to no less than twenty lines of the commentary being devoted to the significance of the word 'tower', as in 'Ludlow tower', which, although mentioned three times in 'The Recruit' (ASL III), is a word that occurs only once again in the entire series, namely in 'chiming tower' of XXXVII. In a letter written in the 1920s, presumably to a young poet, Housman wrote:

> Do not ever read books about versification: no poet ever learnt that way. If you are going to be a poet, it will come to you naturally and you will pick up all you need from reading poetry.

Theodore Watts-Dunton[25] took the liberty of classifying poetic imagination into two types: (1) 'absolute dramatic vision . . . unconditioned by the personal or lyrical impulses of the poet' (exemplified by Aeschylus, Sophocles, Shakespeare and Homer); and (2) 'relative dramatic vision (which) is poetry more or less conditioned by the personal or lyrical impulse of the poet' (exemplified by Pindar, Dante, Milton, Sappho, Heine and Shelley). Housman clearly belongs to the second category, although in his greatest philosophical moments – albeit moments of great scepticism – when the world is the backdrop to universal truths and when his tenderness breaks through into comparative magnanimity, he makes a gallant attempt to see life 'steadily' and to see life 'whole', as Arnold said of Sophocles. For in his intimate affection for soil and scenery Housman's Arcadian spirit is willingly dragged downward by thoughts of malign reversals both of nature and of the universe itself.

In Housman's verse translations of some of Sophocles's tragedies,[26] he employs consciously antiquated language for effect, and one can find striking similarities between the outlook of the two poets. First the Sophoclean chorus in a particularly sombre mood:

> Thy portion esteem I highest,
> Who wast not ever begot;
> Thine next, being born who diest
> And straightway again art not.[27]

I regard this as the most futile of pessimisms and the most fallacious of reasoning. Now Housman's gloom which, I admit, is gracefully put:

> Then came I crying, and to-day,
> With heavier cause to plain,
> Depart I into death away,
> Not to be born again.

(MP XXV)

Sophocles was talking of Oedipus, the tragic figure *par*

excellence; Housman however is preoccupied with his own inner sorrow and possibly exercising his skills as a sort of Anglo-Latinist. In MP II, Housman, lyrical, morose and ultimately pedantic, makes no attempt to shape his own destiny. The last two verses, which follow the Old Testament stories about God's care of the Children of Israel when emerging from exile, run:

> The realm I look upon and die
> Another man will own;
> He shall attain the heaven that I
> Perish and have not known.
>
> But I will go where they are hid
> That never were begot,
> To my inheritance amid
> The nation that is not.

Another similarly terse conclusion makes an appearance of the end of another poem which he again held back from publication during his lifetime:

> There in their graves my comrades are,
> In my grave I am not.
>
> (MP XXXIX)

Notice how, in MP II, Housman's use of 'enjambments' in the second half of each stanza reduces the jingling quality. This effect is more obvious in the poem selected by Laurence as the prefatory poem for *More Poems* which gives warning of what lies in store for us. The second verse, here quoted, shows the tightest of clipped lines in a balanced inversion of metre. Here is more than a dash of Sophoclean tragedy, but this in contrast embodies a degree of sympathy for those yet to be born:

72

> This is for all ill-treated fellows
> Unborn and unbegot,
> For them to read when they're in trouble
> And I am not.

Arnold, remember, felt like a wanderer 'between two worlds, one dead,/The other powerless to be born'. As if to imbed this habit, the last line of every stanza in MP XXXIV shortens the metre, which successfully enhances the dignity of each stanza in turn. It ends:

> Young is the blood that yonder
> Succeeds to rick and fold,
> Fresh are the form and favour
> And new the minted mould:
> The thoughts are old.

Housman is consistent in his wish to reach out to those 'ill-treated' fellows. That excellent Sophoclean dedication, tinged with Housman's sardonic humour, extends the same wishes as were heard in the valedictory poem of *A Shropshire Lad*. It is a real effort to 'harmonize the sadness',[28] if not of the universe, then of a rejected poet's life and others rejected in love:

> I hoed and trenched and weeded,
> And took the flowers to fair:
> I brought them home unheeded;
> The hue was not the wear.
>
> So up and down I sow them
> For lads like me to find,
> When I shall lie below them,
> A dead man out of mind.
>
> Some seed the birds devour,
> And some the season mars,
> But here and there will flower
> The solitary stars,

>And fields will yearly bear them
>As light-leaved spring comes on,
>And luckless lads will wear them
>When I am dead and gone.

>(ASL LXIII)

The poem can be compared with the Parable of the Sower: '. . . and the fowls of the air came and devoured (the seed) up' and 'but when the sun was up, (the seed) was scorched'.[29] It is an allegorical poem in the strict sense which plays too much with grief to merit comparison with Sophocles's *gravitas*. The metre is simple, the message plain. A pleasant minor chord on which to end leaves one satisfied though not satiated. To most late Victorian and Edwardian readers, 'luckless lads' was referring to men steeped in perplexity about their atheism, their homosexuality, or both. The beauty of the lyrics is that the lucklessness might as readily have been caused by anything, and could be taken to refer to anything, or nothing.

In 1879 the young Housman wrote a prize-winning poem, called 'Iona', based on some lines of Catullus. Like the Roman poet, Housman was to see flaws in the institution of marriage. For instance, he wrote this wedding song for Moses, beginning:

>He is here, Urania's son,
>Hymen come from Helicon;
>God that glads the lover's heart,
>He is here to join and part.

>(LP XXIV)

Now the emotional Catullus, chanting his strange marriage song in the last passionate phrase:

Collis o Heliconii
  culter, Uraniae genus,
qui rapis tenerum ad virum
Virginem, O Hymenaee Hymen,
  O Hymen, Hymenaee.

Catullus would readily have understood the kind of love Housman bore for Moses Jackson:

Difficile est longum subito deponere amorem.
[*It is difficult suddenly to lay aside a long love.*]

Housman's voice was of a retiring kind; poetry for him was, again, a 'secretion like turpentine in the fir; or a morbid secretion, like the pearl in the oyster'.[30] It appealed, and appeals still to a vast readership but, however narrative it becomes, as in 'Hell Gate' (LP XXXI), is still poetry of Watts-Dunton's 'egotism', that is, intensely personal in origin. 'A.J.J.' was written of his dear friend Adalbert, Moses Jackson's brother, and was too personal, like MP XXX – about Moses – to be published in his lifetime. Again there is a mundane, matter-of-fact closing line to the first stanza of 'A.J.J.' – practical, without profundity, but redeemed by its resigned quality:

When he's returned I'll tell him – oh,
Dear fellow, I forgot:
Time was you would have cared to know,
But now it matters not.

(MP XLII)

The older he became the more hermetically Housman sealed the windows against the fresh air from the 'west land'. In *Last Poems* he wallowed in the humid marshes of introspection; I count only about five of the forty-one

poems as being more about landscape than doom.
Whole brigades of soldiery are wiped out in *Last Poems*
in moments of deep egoism. Ludlow's tower does man-
age briefly to rise again above the marsh-gas, but the
poem, LP XXXIV, was completed in 1905 and may well
have been conceived even earlier. In this poem, 'The
First of May', the rhythm of spring's annual arrival, to
which the fair held at Ludlow each year on 1 May pays
tribute, corresponds with a new batch from a generation younger and equally doomed. It is a very gentle
scepticism. The last verse might be read as a sigh from
an older, wiser Ludlovian. The archaic 'Ay, yonder'
helps to distance youth from old age – as it does in
Romeo and Juliet: 'The pretty wretch left crying, and said
"Ay"':

> Ay, yonder lads are yet
> The fools that we were then;
> For oh, the sons we get
> Are still the sons of men.
> The sumless tale of sorrow
> Is all unrolled in vain:
> May comes to-morrow
> And Ludlow fair again.

(LP XXXIV)

To rhyme with 'stay' Housman, excusably, uses the
word 'aye' (MP XLV); he first did this in his translation
of Horace's 'Diffugere Nives' (MP V), repeating the line
in the preceding 'The Sage to the Young Man' (MP IV):
'Thou wast not born for aye', which resonates with
Keats' 'Thou was not born for death, immortal Bird!'.[31]

Housman was able to cater for the demand for
nostalgia in Victorian England by using country people,
and to relate misfortune and comradeship to the shared

tribulations and trials of fighting; but it was left to Wilfred Owen (1893–1918) and Edward Thomas (1878–1917), to name but two, to paint the true picture of a world war's carnage. Thomas, unlike Housman, was sensitive enough to realise that the Great War would mark the end of an epoch. Housman looked back over both fresh graves in country churchyards and battlegrounds in his search for wisdom for others; Thomas looked out over the vast ranks of fresh war graves to confront the spirit of change itself. Stylistically Thomas's contribution to modern poetry was that, like Robert Frost and Thomas Hardy, he ignored nineteenth-century poeticisms in favour of using everyday language. None of them would have written words like these by Housman:

> Up, lad: thews that lie and cumber
> Sunlit pallets never thrive;
> Morns abed and daylight slumber
> Were not meant for man alive.
>
> (ASL IV)

To be fair to Housman, however, although he was not using dialect to defend the use of antiquated language, such speech is still to be heard from older people in the Yorkshire Dales. ('Dost tha noa owt or nowt about yonder clarty do?' was asked of me the other day.) Housman's poem could possibly be rendered in a deep, lyrical Shropshire voice from the farmyard. Strangely for a classicist, he preferred early Gothic to Classical architecture – he never visited Greece – and resorted to 'early' words rather than to flowery Victorianisms. He used the soft word 'lief' derived from 'love', in its usual meaning of 'willingly', or as it used to be in Victorian days, 'lovingly':

> Could man be drunk for ever
> With liquor, love, or fights,
> Lief should I rouse at morning
> And lief lie down of nights.
>
> (LP X)

'O' or 'Oh' is a good opportunity for an intake of breath; perhaps that is why in so many lyrics it is tacked on to the front of lines. Many lines in *A Shropshire Lad* begin thus, not as in the vigorous pronouncement 'O God', but more as a waning, tired expletive. 'Oh' beseeches in *Last Poems*: 'Oh who would not sleep with the brave' – lines stolen from William Collins' 'Ode' of 1747:

> How sleep the brave, who sink to rest,
> By all their country's wishes blest!

and as in *A Shropshire Lad* also merely fills in time as an extra syllable – 'Oh I have been to Ludlow fair', or place – 'Oh tarnish late on Wenlock Edge'. Three times in ASL V it accords the iambics their proper rise:

> Oh may I squire you round the meads
> And pick you posies gay?

Similarly Housman was found of ' 'twas', ' 'tis', 'yon' and 'yonder'. As for 'lad' itself, among country people in the remoter parts of the Pennines it is a colloquialism with currency still, usually uttered in a lighthearted, comradely spirit. 'Durst' is now dated, but has a mucky, rustic ring to it, which I imagine was not the original intention:

78

Others, I am not the first,
Have willed more mischief than they durst.

(ASL XXX)

As 'durst' rhymes here with 'first', so 'dost' rhymes
with 'just' in 'The Sage to the Young Man' (MP IV). In
MP XLIV we find:

> From dusty wreck dispersed
> Its stature mounts amain;
> On surer foot than first
> The belfry stands again.

'Amain' means 'with strength' and was a word much
cultivated by Victorian poets. Poetical stratagems such
as 'o'er' to rhyme with 'more' (LP XXIX) are aberrations,
as in the following second half of ASL XLVI. Although
this is stiff with obsolescent words and the last line
poorly scanned, I nevertheless find the poem intelligi-
ble and profound. Housman liked to use flowers as
palliatives – even old 'haulms':

> But if the Christmas field has kept
> Awns the last gleaner overstept,
> Or shrivelled flax, whose flower is blue
> A single season, never two;
> Or if one haulm whose year is o'er
> Shivers on the upland frore,
> – Oh, bring from hill and stream and plain
> Whatever will not flower again,
> To give him comfort: he and those
> Shall bide eternal bedfellows
> Where low upon the couch he lies
> Whence he never shall arise.

(ASL XLVI)

The mood could scarcely be more different from the one Euripides evoked: 'He sat in the meadow and plucked with glad heart the spoil of the flowers, gathering them one by one.' In its evocation of a barren, sleet-swept hillside, 'Shivers on the upland frore' is most apposite.

To the question 'Is my team ploughing', Housman's lad answers 'ay', which, like 'lad' itself, is common in northern speech and no doubt also a west country, indeed a widely used word for 'yes'. Housman is fond of 'lours', a word frequently encountered in the poetry of his day. The word 'blithe' crops up in *A Shropshire Lad* and twice in 'God's Acre':

> Blithe the maids to milking, blithe
> Men in hayfields stone the scythe.
>
> (AP XI)

The word is defined as 'gay' and 'joyous' in most dictionaries and is most apt for 'maids' in the arcadian world of Housman's poetry, further emphasising the lad's contrasting gloom – a gloom which strangely never drags the poems down so that they read like dirges. Housman's natural humour, confidence in his skills won in such places as the British Museum during his Patent Office days, and his cynicism won in the struggle to overcome trauma, are the miscellaneous ingredients for an odd ragout of morbidity.

Thus I find 'The Immortal Part', with its biblical appendages 'hearken' and 'travail', and two each of 'flesh' and 'soul', has a more uplifting effect than is usual in morbid contemplative poetry of this kind:

> When I meet the morning beam
> Or lay me down at night to dream,
> I hear my bones within me say,
> 'Another night, another day.'
>
> (ASL XLIII)

By the end of this poem the original weariness of the lad's toil has been resolved and the 'bones' rally:

> Therefore they shall do my will
> To-day while I am master still, . . .

At the day's end, thirteen poems below, the light is switched off, the poet closes the door and, mulling over the toil of loving, he sighs with a hint of self-satisfaction:

> 'Tis late to hearken, late to smile,
> But better late than never:
> I shall have lived a little while
> Before I die for ever.
>
> (ASL LVII)

This is on the same lines as Tennyson's:

> 'Tis better to have loved and lost
> Than never to have loved at all.

Last Poems X, which employs the word 'lief', ends with a theatrical gesture that is a veritable masterstroke, 'think' becoming almost interchangeable with 'drink':

> Could man be drunk for ever
> With liquor, love, or fights,
> Lief should I rouse at morning
> And lief lie down of nights.
>
> But men at whiles are sober
> And think by fits and starts,
> And if they think, they fasten
> Their hands upon their hearts.

To summarise, Housman's prosody, within his general mastery of rhythmic techniques, exhibits a preference for the spondee in a basic iambic rhythm and for combining and inverting the iambic with the trochaic foot. He is fond of feminine endings, counterpointed rhythms and the classical epigram; and he is fondest above all of mid-Victorian romantic poetry. The largest single source of references in his poetry is the Old Testament; there are some from Latin poets, and a few from lesser earlier Victorian poets like G. A. Simcox. He also owed a debt to Shakespheare's songs, Milton, Border Balladeers, Scott, Blake[32] Tennyson, Keats, Arnold and lesser figures such as Robert Louis Stevenson as poet. The late Philip Larkin once correctly remarked: 'Perhaps there was more of a mid-Victorian in Housman than is generally realised.'

'He never blotted a word', it was said of Shakespeare to which Ben Jonson commented, 'Would he had blotted a thousand'. Housman himself scorned the alteration of poems once they had been completed and published. Wordsworth was a prime tinkerer, whereas Housman made only two 'corrections' after publication. These were both in *A Shropshire Lad*, and the alterations were made at the time of publication of *Last Poems* twenty-six years after that of *A Shropshire Lad*. They are: 'loose on the wind' in place of 'thick on the wind' (XXXVIII) and, more poignantly, 'no more remembered' for 'long since forgotten' (LII). They are lovely words and, because they are familiar and uncomplicated words, not strongly metaphoric, they appear simple. In that sense Housman is a master of evocation through simplicity. But the single-mindedness of his message is far from monotonous once one delves into the rich variety of rhythms with which he expertly handles words, and the many stages on which he places his characters so that they may utter them. Horace, in *Ars Poetica*, wrote: 'You may gain the finest effects in language by the skilful setting which makes a well known word new.'

Housman tried not only to understand the predicament of 'luckless lads', but made great efforts to reach them with his palliatives and advice:

> You smile upon your friend to-day,
> To-day his ills are over;
> You hearken to the lovers' say,
> And happy is the lover.
>
> 'Tis late to hearken, late to smile,
> But better late than never:
> I shall have lived a little while
> Before I die forever.
>
> (ASL LVII)

Nowhere is the yearning so fervent as in MP XXX, presumably too personal for him to publish during his lifetime. It was begun a year or so earlier and finished in June 1895. Even when deep in sorrow over his separation from Moses Jackson, Housman was sufficiently generous for it to be kindness and love that was allowed to emerge. If the last line harks back to Burns's hillsong 'O whistle and I'll come to you' (and from 'Auld Lang Syne' we rejoin 'And there's a hand, my trusty fiere, / And gie's a hand o' thine . . .'), the wistful second verse is uniquely Housman's:

> Shake hands, we shall never be friends, all's over;
> I only vex you the more I try.
> All's wrong that ever I've done or said,
> And nought to help it in this dull head:
> Shake hands, here's luck, good-bye.
>
> But if you come to a road where danger
> Or guilt or anguish or shame's to share,
> Be good to the lad that loves you true
> And the soul that was born to die for you,
> And whistle and I'll be there.[33]
>
> (MP XXX)

This is commitment; it is also an impassioned gesture which, in the form of immortal verse, is offered to future generations. What more could Housman offer?

NOTES

1. Wordsworth, Preface to *Lyrical Ballads*, 1800.
2. The Name and Nature of Poetry, in *Selected Prose*, ed. John Carter (CUP, 1961).
3. Preface to Manilius V.
4. Although not one major composer has set a Housman lyric to music since 1945, 'Loveliest of Trees' (ASL II) was set to music ten times before then.
5. Twelfth Night, Act II, scene iv [58].
6. Ibid., scene iii [50].
7. *Hamlet*, Act II, scene ii [115].
8. *Cymbeline*, IV, ii.
9. *Aeniad*, Bk V, stanza LXXIV/lines 539–40.
10. Wordsworth, Preface to *Lyrical Ballads* (1798; enlarged edn 1800).
11. All these names are often used in English pastoral poetry.
12. ASL XXXVII, L and LI.
13. Letter to Seymour Adelman, 6.5.28, recorded by Laurence Housman, *A.E.H.* Also *Letters*, p. 264.
14. Letter to M. Pollet, 5.2.33.
15. From Matthew Arnold's essay *Heinrich Heine*.
16. Quoted in *An Anthology of World Poetry* (Cassell, 1929).
17. Letter to Witter Bynner, 3.6.03. *Letters*, p. 63.
18. Letter to J. W. Mackail, 25.7.22. MS Fitzwilliam Museum, Cambridge. *Letters*, p. 200.
19. 'It is worth noting that most of the finest of his poems came with most difficulty, or anyway were subjected to most correction'. *A.E.H.*, p. 253.
20. 'Men are sick with love:' (last lines of Blake's 'The Vision of Beulah'); nothing beats 'To Thy high requiem become a sod' (Keats, 'Ode to a Nightingale') as an unmeant joke.
21. *A Midsummer Night's Dream*, Act IV, scene i, l. 102.

PICNICKING TENTH-CENTURY PERSIAN POETS, from a manuscript
painting (detail) in the Shah-nameh of Shah Tahmasp (reproduced by kind
permission of Prince Sadruddin Aga Khan)

CORNFIELD BY MOONLIGHT WITH THE EVENING STAR, from a wash
drawing by Samuel Palmer (*by kind permission of the Trustees of the
British Museum*)

ST AUGUSTINE IN HIS STUDY, detail from the fresco by Sandro Botticelli

MAN AND WOMAN GAZING AT THE MOON, from the painting by
Caspar David Friedrich (*by kind permission of the Nationalgalerie, Berlin*)

22. ASL XXXII/XXXIII; and LIX/LX.

23. Letter to Mackail (Ibid).

24. Ed. Tomio Suzuki (Aratake: Tokyo).

25. 1832–1914; critic, novelist, poet and friend to, and possible saviour of, Swinburne. It is amusing to read in *A.E.H.* that Housman's landlady interviewed a cook who had just come from that position with Watts-Dunton and Swinburne. These two had driven her to exhaustion by wanting food at two in the morning in order to keep the poetry coming!

26. From *Odes from the Greek Dramatists*, ed. Alfred Pollard, transl. A. E. Housman (David Stott, 1890).

27. From *Oedipus at Coloneus*, lines 1225–30; these particular lines repr. in *Collected Poems of A. E. Housman* (Cape, 1967).

28. Letter to Katherine Symons, 5.10.15. M/S Lilly Library, Indiana. *Letters*, p. 140.

29. Mark, IV, 4, 6.

30. Leslie Stephen Lecture, 1933.

31. 'Ode to a Nightingale', stanza 7.

32. William Blake was rightly considered by Housman to be the most poetical of poets and as one of those whose 'elements of their natures were more or less insurgent against the centralised tyranny of the intellect' (from Housman's 1933 Lecture, The Name and Nature of Poetry).

33. There is a west-country legend called 'Whistle and I'll come to you' ('Oh, Whistle and I'll Come to You, My Lad' is the title of M. R. James' 1904 ghost story). While Housman stayed with the Hardys at Max Gate near Dorchester he may have picked up the legend, although he seems always to have read ghost stories with relish.

4 · HARDY, SAPPHO, THE RUBÁIYÁT AND STARS

And foreign constellations west
Each night above his mound.
Thomas Hardy, *Drummer Hodge*

HOUSMAN AND HARDY

In the same way as Housman paradoxically hid a loving and sympathetic heart beneath a stiff and starchy exterior, Hardy, too, though socially more at ease than Housman, was reserved and exhibited similar traits that belied an intensely poetic imagination. Many of Hardy's poems have as strong an identity and sombre a tone as Housman's, but with more variation in metre and more experimentation. Both men wrote poetry because, preoccupied with the unexplained and the painful, they were provoked, as the best artists may be, both by the strange wonder of the miniscule and by what Hardy called the 'tragical mystery'. They shared the urge to express the cruel side of life; they were strongly conditioned by personal impulse.

If Hardy spotted a tiny moth or beetle[1] or Housman came across a primrose in 'hollow ground'[2] they focused their imaginations with the same intense concentration, as if they were imagining the firmament immobilised by Fate itself. In conjunction with such sympathies, they encapsulated an identical love of all things rural, noting the effects of the seasons and, in Hardy's case in particular, expressing profound sorrow at the changes wrought by mankind itself on country ways. A. Alvarez thus wrote of *Tess of the D'Urbervilles*:

> In a way the tragedy of Tess, a pure woman, is also
> the tragedy of the old, 'pure' Wessex from which she
> comes. Both are corrupted and betrayed by the mod-
> ern world in its various aspects . . . '.[3]

This was a vision that Housman did not entirely share;
indeed Ludlow Tower, pointedly, is taken as a symbol
of the immutable backdrop that remains while Ludlow
lads go off to fight and die, or perhaps return, as in 'The
Recruit' (ASL III). However, since Hardy and Housman
both grew up in the country, when they introduced
'Nature' it never over-rode the human predicament but
fused with it; thus, particularly with Hardy, both landscape and person became bonded. Mankind was pre-
dominantly viewed as a puny creature, living in a
universe that appeared indifferent:

> Nature is played out as a Beauty, but not as a Mystery
> . . . I don't want to see the original realities – as optical
> effects, that is. I want to see the deeper reality under-
> lying the scenic, the expression of what are some-
> times called abstract imaginings.

Hardy's words are in tune with Housman. They also
shared common experiences of disappointment in love
– Hardy's long first marriage was hardly blissful – and a
sense of life's injustice. They were both stoical in the
face of their ordeals and were both moved by the great
poetry in the Bible. Both were fatalists, though Hardy's
adamant stand against Fate is very different from Housman's acceptance of it.

When Housman wrote, 'Is my team ploughing'
(ASL XXVII) he was not concerned with the prospect of
some new invention taking over the horses' tasks; he

was evoking the continuity of certain ways of life, and even the 'ways' of a young ploughman's widow. Its treatment of the topic of fickleness among women was one of the reasons why, according to the first Mrs Hardy, this was her husband's favourite among the poems in *A Shropshire Lad*. Around the fragile core of sorry human predicaments Housman could skilfully wrap pretty tissue paper soaked in nostalgia for the countryside; the nostalgia was evoked not because it might or might not occur, but because it was simply no longer immediately accessible. That is why Housman imprisoned Shropshire-bred Terence in London which in 1896 was still a slow train journey away from Ludlow.

On the other hand, Hardy's nostalgia rested in the change itself: he loved the old country ways in which he was brought up. His second book, *Under the Greenwood Tree*, was a kind of 'Shropshire Lad' novel without so must *angst*, while his ever-popular novel *Tess of the D'Urbervilles*, published nineteen years later in 1891 – five years before *A Shropshire Lad* – has at its heart an abundance of this sense of primal sadness. *The Mayor of Casterbridge* presents cameos of the vanished Arcadia of rural England, which affect the feelings of its characters and their conduct towards each other. The last words of the book are: 'Happiness was but the occasional episode in a general drama of pain.'

The poetical expressions of both authors were strongly coloured – or discoloured – by melancholia; each possessed the power to be at the same time concerned with tragedy and detached from it by the cynicism that distorted their viewpoint. Rarely did Housman write a poem within a month of whatever intensely felt episode had provoked it. By enduring griefs, facing and rationalising them, Housman was able to impart a kind of wistful consistency to his voice.

Hardy, the older by nearly twenty years, met Housman in 1899 at one of the dinner-parties held by the literary critic Edmund Gosse at his London house. Soon afterwards, as they had then established a rapport, Hardy invited Housman down to stay with him at Max Gate near Dorchester. In 1913[4] and 1914 they were both guests of Sydney Cockerell for dinners at Jesus College, Cambridge. Second perhaps to Jane Austen, Housman liked Hardy most of all novelists. Five years after Hardy's death and three years before his own, he went further: 'For Hardy I felt affection and high admiration for some of his novels and a few of his poems.'[5] Two years later in another letter we read 'Hardy and I never talked about my poems'[6], which explains why it was left to Mrs Hardy to disclose to Housman which was her husband's favourite among the poems in *A Shropshire Lad*. This lack of discussion about poetry may seem odd, but here were two very private 'souls', both extremely reserved, and there was perhaps too much risk of raw nerve-ends being touched.

It is known that Housman thought Bridges and Hardy too prolific. He sent copies of the newly published *Last Poems* to each, as well as to John Masefield and John Drinkwater. While Bridges is a poet of the morning, Housman is a poet of evening, and Hardy is a poet of the night. Housman probably wrote his midnight poem 'The Isle of Portland' (ASL LIX) in the summer of 1894. His inclusion of this poem among the Shropshire cycle was probably an act of homage to Hardy, even though he did not actually meet him until about 1899. More to the point, knowing which of the poems in *A Shropshire Lad* Hardy most liked, it is not inconceivable that Hardy was prompted by that poem to have voices 'of souls of the felled' questioning him. Indeed verse X of 'The Souls of the Slain' describes the conduct of a mourning sweetheart as a precise counterpart to that of the Shropshire ploughman's girl:

> 'And, General, how hold out our sweethearts,
> Sworn loyal as doves?'
> – 'Many mourn; many think
> It is not unattractive to prink
> Them in sables for heroes. Some fickle and
>   fleet hearts
> Have found them new loves.'

I shall be demonstrating some other similarities between Housman's and Hardy's poems, as well as further subtle differences in their outlooks. The dour 'felon-quarried stone', for instance, of Housman's 'Isle' (ASL LIX), so distinct from the usual 'summer fields' of Shropshire, has the same macabre weight of Hardy's Portland Bill poem. While in ASL IX Housman has remained on home ground with an obvious allusion to his original Terence Hearsay idea (in the previous poem might be thought the cause for the hanging at Shrewsbury), he now looks a great deal further 'from moonlit heath and lonesome bank' to 'yonder island' and the grave of another of his criminal friends. The location of a prison may have been selected to exemplify man's shackled state during life, and his release in death, but there is again a strong nostalgic element. The lines

> Far from his folk a dead lad lies
> That once was friends with me

explain that the criminal was from Shropshire, probably having committed murder, and had been hanged. As in 'The Carpenter's Son' (ASL XLVII) with its strong allusion to the momentous events on Calvary, the poignancy is enhanced because he has died so far from home. The unfairness of the sentence, or the iniquity of the process of execution, do not concern Housman in *A Shropshire Lad*. Presuming Laurence's annotation of his brother's notebooks to be correct, the Portland poem was written in the latter half of 1894 and the first draft of the Shrewsbury jail poem soon after in February 1895.

In April 1895 Oscar Wilde most unwisely brought the libel action against the Marquis of Queensbury, which was to ruin both his career and health. Thus while these two prison poems show no reference to Wilde's unfortunate predicament and while 'The Carpenter's Son', written in August 1895, also lacks such an allusion, the prisoner in AP XVIII who has been jailed for 'the colour of his hair', refers to Wilde in Reading prison. Housman obviously did not want to risk controversy by publishing it himself. 'Steadfast stars', as Heine called them, take no sides: they shine equally on prisons and on graves and will shine on seas when all controversy has ceased and prisons and graves are gone:

> The star-filled seas are smooth to-night
> From France to England strown;
> Black towers above the Portland light
> The felon-quarried stone.

> (ASL LIX)

One learns little more about Portland Bill from Hardy even after ninety-six lines stemming from a December night's contemplation when

> Alone at the Bill
> Of the Isle by the race.

'The race' results from the meeting of contrary tides,

and in those perpetually troubled waters Hardy sees thousands of ghostly soldiers who beseech the poet for news of their families. Housman does not strive after such grand ideas; he ends IX saying that he will

> . . . wish my friend as sound a sleep
> As lads' I did not know . . .

and the 'Isle' poem with

> Lie you easy, dream you light,
> And sleep you fast for aye;
> And luckier may you find the night
> Than ever you found the day.

The following compassionate reverie is Hardy at his most reflective:

> Yonder a maid and her wight
> Come whispering by:
> War's annals will cloud into night
> Ere their story die.

'In Time of "The Breaking of Nations"', from which that was the last stanza, has a wistfulness, a well-ordered scansion that precludes fast reading, employs archaic language to suggest timelessness – by 'wight' Hardy meant man – and rises from thoughts of the simplest kind to those eternal truths which 'harmonise' our sadnesses. Here is Housman with practical advice for the bachelor brother of that 'wight' – lines more direct than Hardy's, in which we instantly recognise his brand of melancholy pessimism:

> Now hollow fires burn out to black,
> And lights are guttering low:

Square your shoulders, lift your pack,
And leave your friends and go.

Oh never fear, man, nought's to dread,
Look not left nor right:
In all the endless road you tread
There's nothing but the night.

(ASL LX)

Regarding poetic diction, take these slightly Hop-
kinsian lines from Hardy's 'The Five Students':

The sparrow dips in his wheel-rut bath,
The sun grows passionate-eyed,
And boils the dew to smoke by paddock-path.

Housman occasionally used such word clusters, though
his metaphors were in general conjured up with few
words: 'Steeple-shadowed slumber', 'cloud-led shadows', 'star-defeated sighs' and 'valley-guarded
granges'. He was the master of emphasis, even though
on occasion he appears mundane and prosaic: 'There's
nothing but the night'.

While Hardy and Housman could both write
poetry like Kipling, when burying soldiers as if in
mockery of death, Housman was the more sensitive: he
would not have minded sharing the soldier's grave. His
brother, who had been a particularly brave soldier, had
met his death in war and if Housman mocks, he is at the
same time very sad, as he drums out the pathos and
horror which can result when following the 'King and
Country' code:

Farewell to a name and a number,
Recalled again
To darkness and silence and slumber
In blood and pain.

So ceases and turns to the thing
He was born to be
A soldier cheap to the King
And dear to me;

So smothers in blood the burning
And flaming flight
Of valour and truth, returning
To dust and night.

(MP XL)

The blackbird in ASL VII is nesting (in spirit) close
by Hardy's 'ecstatic sounding' darkling thrush[7] and
Keats's 'ecstatic' darkling nightingale. But while Hardy
himself is puzzled at such 'carolings' in the desolation
of a darkening winter's evening, Housman's ploughman is more likely to silence the songbird with a well-
aimed stone because the repetitive mocking lyric so
annoys him as he strides 'against the morning beam'.
Hardy and Keats loved their birds. Housman, apart
from this hapless 'blackbird in the coppice', introduces
'ravens' in 'The Welsh Marches' as a symbol of death in
war; otherwise he seems impervious to bird or animal
life. This is strange, but serves to emphasise yet further
his preoccupation with the unenviable 'lot' of man. (His
attitude to dumb creatures may be inferred from stories
that he kicked dogs out of his path.)

This contrast in the focus and the intensity of
emotions is also seen when comparing the coffinless
Drummer Hodge's undignified burial mound and the
tombstones of Shropshire soldiers who also died hun-
dreds of miles from their homes. Hardy does not grow
indignant or embittered by the pity of it all: he stands
aloof like a journalist recording names of those attend-
ing a funeral. There is a similar contrast between the
response of Housman's lad in the 'Grecian gallery' of

ASL LI and the character in Hardy's 'In the British Museum'. Remarkably similar to a Housman poem, however, which may suggest that Housman 'lifted' the idea, are the lines in *Tess* which run:

> The shabby corner of God's allotment where he lets the nettles grow, and where all . . . suicides, and others of the conjecturally damned are laid.

Here is the opening stanza of Housman's poem:

> It nods and curtseys and recovers
> When the wind blows above,
> The nettle on the graves of lovers
> That hanged themselves for love.
>
> (ASL XVI)

Hardy certainly wished to be remembered as 'a man who used to notice such things. Those words come from his own elegy entitled 'Afterwards', where, after showing in the first stanza how his curiosity was aroused by the miniscule, by the fourth stanza Hardy is raking among the stars for clues regarding secrets far beyond the earth:

> If, when hearing that I have been stilled at last,
>   they stand at the door,
> Watching the full-starred heavens that winter sees,
> Will this thought rise on those who will meet my
>   face no more,
> 'He was one who had an eye for such mysteries'?

In Hardy's novel, the fantasy *Two on a Tower*, a character warns: 'It is better – far better – for me to forget the Universe than to bear it clearly in mind.' Housman nods in agreement – while shining as an epigrammatist:

> Here are the skies, the planets seven,
> And all the starry train;
> Content you with the mimic heaven,
> And on the earth remain.[8]

(AP V)

It is necessary to quote no more than the last verse of Hardy's 'Drummer Hodge', to see the stars as moving eyes, at which we can likewise stare back, to be either comforted by their familiarity or disturbed by the eternal enigma of their awesome presence. They are hardly to be blamed, yet Housman writes: 'The stars have not dealt me the worst they could do . . .' (AP XVII).Describing the Wessex soldier's miserable burial in the 'broad karoo' of Boer country, Hardy merely notes the difference between stars of the nothern and southern climes:

> Yet portion of that unknown plain
> Will Hodge for ever be;
> His homely Northern breast and brain
> Grow to some Southern tree,
> And strange-eyed constellations reign
> His stars eternally.[9]

These are, nevertheless, feelings of compassion, with which, back on his home territory of Wessex in *Tess*, he could more deeply identify:

A field-man is a personality afield; a field-woman is a portion of the field; she has somehow lost her own margin, imbibed the essence of her surrounding, and assimilated herself with it.

It was no accident that Hardy called his dead drummer 'Hodge' for in the nineteenth century 'Hodge', derived from Roger, was a familiar nickname for a farm labourer. This was certainly so in southern England, though in the poem quoted above it is associated by Hardy with the 'Northern (*European*) breast'. Is this, in ASL XXXV, the ghost of Drummer Hodge transferred to Shropshire, resting on a hilltop alone under the midday sun?

> On the idle hill of summer,
> Sleepy with the flow of streams,
> Far I hear the steady drummer
> Drumming like a noise in dreams.

And has Sergeant Troy[10] mightily disturbed the day-dream?

> Far the calling bugles hollo,
> High the screaming fife replies . . .

And are these the remains of Housman's soldiers that answer the call?

> East and west on fields forgotten
> Bleach the bones of comrades slain.

With his eyes cast downwards and his feet firmly on Dorset soil, Hardy, like Housman, unable to solve the enigma of the heavens, thought of 'ill-treated fellows / 'Unborn and unbegot', as he wrote the pitiful 'To an Unborn Pauper Child', knowing he was powerless in the face of such calamities:

> But I am weak as thou and bare;
> No man can change the common lot to rare.

97

Or as Housman put it:

> Stars, I have seen them fall,
> But when they drop and die
> No star is lost at all
> From all the star-sown sky.
> The toil of all that be
> Helps not the primal fault;
> It rains into the sea,
> And still the sea is salt.

> (MP VII)

When Hardy died in 1928, Housman was among the distinguished pallbearers – with Shaw, Gosse, Barrie, Kipling, Galsworthy and one serving prime minister Baldwin and (soon to be his successor) Ramsay Macdonald – who carried the coffin at the funeral in Westminster Abbey.

HOUSMAN AND SAPPHO

> Love, like a mountain-wind upon an oak,
> Falling upon me, shakes the leaf and bough.
> Sappho (fragment transl. by W. E. Leonard)

There is a legend that Sappho, who lived in the seventh century BC, was made so wretched by an unrequited love affair that she leaped from the Leucadian rock, a promontory on the island of Leucas in the Ionian Sea from which such sufferers often resolved their troubles., The more likely story is that she left Lesbos for political reasons, and went to Sicily around 600 BC. Her love for Phaon the boatman must be one of the longest-running, unrequited love stories ever.

If we know little about the events of her life, we know much more about her character than that of Theocritus, as she wrote out her feelings in superb, emotional lyrics that have come down to us in generous measure when compared with the mere fragments that remain of many other prolific ancients. In all, we have nine books of her verse, which once contained almost a thousand lines each. Of these, four books consist of no more than fragments; only about a dozen poems seem so far to have survived. Whereas Homer was known as 'The Poet', she was known as 'The Poetess'. Though extraordinarily passionate, she was said to be short and dark, so it may have been her verses rather than her looks that earned her the epithet of 'The Beauty' during classical times. Her technique was faultless and her invention of the sapphic metre, among others, was a great gift to poetry. Thomas Campion, the Elizabethan poet, and William Cowper, slightly younger than Thomas Gray, applied the sapphic to English verse. Gray wrote Latin sapphics, the most beautiful being inspired by his return, in the winter of 1740, from Tuscany to London, where he felt a stranger in his own country – much as the Shropshire lad was to feel.

ASL XLI and LII both described such a sense of isolation, the first of these beginning:

> In my own shire, if I was sad,
> Homely comforters I had:
> The earth, because my heart was sore,
> Sorrowed for the son she bore;
> And standing hills, long to remain,
> Shared their short-lived comrade's pain.

Robert Southey's sapphics recall the sentiments – though not of course the metre – in the last verse of ASL XXXVIII, with its 'sigh upon the road':

The wind and I, we both were there,
But neither long abode;
Now through the friendless world we fare
And sigh upon the road.

Now Southey:

Cold was the/night wind,/drifting/fast the/snow fell,
Wide were the/downs and/shelter/less and/naked,
When a poor/wand'rer/struggled/on her/journey,
    Weary and/waysore.

This is hardly Hardy's 'maid and her wight' but a picture of a woman pelted by a pitiless, very unfriendly storm.

Housman was too much the balladeer to employ awkward rhythms in his English poems. Horace used sapphics, with only minor adaptation, in his Odes; and Housman thought Ode IV in Book Seven 'the most beautiful poem in ancient literature'. His translation, 'Diffugere Nives', in *More Poems*, is written in iambic pentameters which lend it a characteristic Latin formality.

The following beautiful fragment of Sappho's verse in translation, is usually entitled 'Alone' or 'I Sleep Alone':

The moon and seven Pleiades have set;
It is the midnight now; the hours go by;
And still I'm lying in my bed alone.

Housman naturally knew these simple words in the original Greek and was clearly very moved by them; he had found a theme to work on, and polish to perfection. In October 1901 he heard that his young brother Herbert had been shot dead in the course of the South African war, and that his body had been lying throughout the night in a puddle that was filling with rain,

'WHISPERING' ASPEN

THE LONG MYND

AN ARCADIA: WENSLEYDALE

'TEAM PLOUGHING'

before it was eventually found. As the Pleiades are stars which would have appeared high in the sky over the South African Veld at the season when they appear low on our own horizon, they would have witnessed Herbert lying in the mud.

> The diamond tears adorning
> Thy low mound on the lea,
> Those are the tears of morning,
> That weeps, but not for thee.

(LP XXVII)

It is typical of Housman to choose 'morning' for 'mourning' since he chose 'thorough' instead of the expected 'through' in ASL XVII.

From about 1900, when he began to emend the bizarre star-worn lines of Manilius's *Astronomica*, Housman began to look to the stars rather than to the hills for inspiration. Even the 'earthy' Theocritus liked stars in his own ebullient way:

But now, when waned the spring, and lambs were fed
 In far-off fields, and Pleiads gleamed o'erhead.[11]

The formation of the Pleiades, the seven brightest stars in the constellation Taurus (in Britain most people see only six with the naked eye on very clear nights), had in classical times been compared to a bunch of grapes. But their name derives rather from a Greek myth, in which Pleione and Atlas had seven daughters who as a result of their grief and tears at the death of their sister, the Hyades, had been transformed into stars. Their lachrymose nature was further recognised in mythology because it was thought to be characteristic of them to rise in mid-May, when the warmer growth-promoting rains fall, and set at the end of October when the autumn gales bring heavy rain. Housman's imagination was

101

fired; what stars could better express the tears of grief, than these Pleiades that are to be seen in both northern and southern skies in November in particular, a mere month after Herbert's death.

The other myth concerning the origin of the Pleiades was that Orion the hunter and his dog saw Pleione and her daughter, and, inflamed with passion, pursued them for five years until Zeus transformed them all into stars. During Theocritus's lifetime, the Book of Job was written, in which there are two references to these stars. With exasperated irony God demands of Job: 'Canst thou bind the sweet influences of Pleiades or loose the bands of Orion?'[12] The 'sweet influences' refer to the stars' rain-bearing qualities and both the Pleiades and Orion (he being supposedly killed by a scorpion) are referred to in three poems by Housman. Omar Khayyám brings together Jupiter and the Pleiades in the following poem ('Parwin' being Persian for the Pleaides):

> I tell you this –
> When, started from the Goal,
> Over the flaming shoulders of the Foal
> Of Heav'n Parwin and Mushtari they flung,
> In my predestin'd Plot of Dust and Soul.[13]

The first of Housman's poems to mention the Pleiades was written in February 1893:

> The weeping Pleiads wester,
> And the moon is under seas;
> From bourn to bourn of midnight
> Far sighs the rainy breeze:
>
> It sighs from a lost country
> To a land I have not known;
> The weeping Pleiads wester,
> And I lie down alone.
>
> (MP X)

Housman's thoughts were probably at the same time borne towards Moses far away in India – 'a land I have not known' – and in Worcestershire, 'a lost country'; this pre-echoes the 'land of lost content' (ASL XL) by which time Housman's attention had switched to Shropshire. It was in November 1892 that Adalbert Jackson had died from typhoid, so it is also likely that the 'land I have not known' was not so much a distant country as a reference to death's abode. The secret of why this poem, with its allusion to the Pleiades, was never included in *A Shropshire Lad*, died with Housman, but it may have been that having the Pleiades shining among the Shropshire poems seemed too obviously of 'classical' derivation.

The next Pleiadic stanzas in *Last Poems*, of which I have quoted half already, were written as a lament for Herbert soon after his death in October 1901. Either because there is such strength of feeling, or because it could sit nobly and conveniently between a 'low' moon (or rather 'half-moon') poem and a 'dreary dawn' poem, Housman inserted it in *Last Poems*:

> The sigh that heaves the grasses
> Whence thou wilt never rise
> Is of the air that passes
> And knows not if it sighs.

> The diamond tears adorning
> Thy low mound on the lea,
> Those are the tears of morning,
> That weeps, but not for thee.

> (LP XXVII)

'The Poetess' would have found no difficulty in making sense of this; the 'diamond tears' are the Pleiades, frequently visible in her sky. They cluster together, but are not particularly bright; they are like the diamonds which Manilius, in G. P. Goold's translation, said 'vie with each other's radiance'. In Britain they may be seen in winter time above the southern horizon.

This next poem, so strongly resembling Sappho's 'Alone', was also written after 1900, but well before *Last Poems* was published, and was perhaps not included in the 1922 volume because of its obvious classical derivation. However, Laurence placed this next to the original 'Pleiadic' poem of 1893, of *More Poems*, which at least facilitates comparison:

> The rainy Pleiads wester,
> Orion plunges prone,
> The stroke of midnight ceases
> And I lie down alone.
>
> The rainy Pleiads wester
> And seek beyond the sea
> The head that I shall dream of
> That will not dream of me.
>
> (MP XI)

One wonders if Housman did not publish 'Diffugere Nives' (MP V) in his lifetime for the same reason, although he thought those lines of Horace among the gems in ancient literature.

Then, like a returning comet, Housman wrote in 1922, especially for publication in *Last Poems*:

> The half-moon westers low, my love,
> And the wind brings up the rain;
> And wide apart lie we, my love,
> And seas between the twain.

It was written for the dying Moses, who for over ten

years had been living near New Westminster in British Columbia. The poem was placed immediately above the previous one written about twenty years before, which is confusing to the student of his verse development. It is hardly surprising that literary critics now tried to identify the departed loved one – who they presumed was a woman – because the poem finishes with the poet muting the clock which originally chimed Sappho's midnight hour. This is the logical conclusion to an old poem about 'rainy', 'weeping Pleiades' (MP X) written in 1893, which had ended 'The weeping Pleiads wester, / And I lie down alone':

> I know not if it rains, my love,
> In the land where you do lie;
> And oh, so sound you sleep, my love,
> You know no more than I.
>
> (LP XXVI)

Housman published one other poem that refers to the stars, though not to the Pleiades. It too was written, like 'Farewell to a name and a number' (MP XL) and 'The rainy Pleiads Wester' (MP XI), about the deeply felt death of his brother in the Boer War. In his curiously titled 'Astronomy', sadness and pathos are expressed through movements of stars in the night sky, significantly that of both hemispheres. Herbert having died in a southern continent, Housman relates in the opening lines how the Great Bear – 'The Wain' – 'descends' from the sky in the southern hemisphere, where, as one looks north, it appears on the horizon in March and April only. Meanwhile the Great Bear remains visible in our northern sky throughout the year. This poem was written within a few months or even weeks of MP XL and MP XI:

The Wain upon the northern steep
Descends and lifts away.
Oh I will sit me down and weep
For bones in Africa.

For pay and medals, name and rank,
Things that he has not found,
He hove the Cross to heaven and sank
The pole-star underground.

And now he does not even see
Signs of the nadir roll
At night over the ground where he
Is buried with the pole.

(LP XVII)

The nadir is the lowest altitude above the horizon to which a star descends during its apparent movement around the earth. The expression therefore found favour in Housman again in '. . . the subterranean dark / Has crossed the nadir, and begins to climb' (LP XXXVI). Illogical as it may seem, this is the sort of phrase which lifts such poetry from depressing dirge into strangely emotive elegy.

The Southern Cross is easily distinguishable, as Housman well knew. In Mediterranean latitudes this constellation is at its lowest elevation in the southern sky during the autumn and winter months. In the southern hemisphere these stars never disappear below the horizon; on the other hand the Pole Star is never visible. In the northern hemisphere, the Pole Star is always visible, bearing due north, and is the star about which the constellations appear to rotate. However, as there is not one equivalent star in the southern hemisphere, we notice how Housman concentrated his attention on the star and the constellation most useful to those who travel great distances in the northern hemisphere – the Pole Star and the Great Bear. (He therefore ignored the Northern Cross which has not much symbolic or practical significance.) Thus Housman, in an amphoteric way, imagines his dying brother seeing, in his death-throes, the Southern Cross rise while he sinks into the grave wherein is already lying his native pole star:

> He hove the Cross to heaven and sank
> The pole-star underground.

LP XVII

Such lines as 'Signs of the nadir roll', from this poem, are open to many interpretations and are the embodiment of Housman's own rule, that it is a physical rather than intellectual approach that produces moving poetry; this was the cornerstone of his last lecture, The Name and Nature of Poetry:

> What is it that can draw tears, as I know it can, to the eyes of more readers than one? What in the world is there to cry about? Why have the mere words the physical effect of pathos when the sense of the passage is blithe and gay? I can only say, because they are poetry, and find their way to something in man which is obscure and latent, something older than the present organisation of his nature, like the patches of fen which still linger here and there in the drained lands of Cambridgeshire.[14]

This last sentence reveals the ease with which Housman can quite effortlessly introduce the landscape – even arcadian – into his thinking.

Heine, the German Romantic whose poetry Housman greatly admired and imitated and who had also suffered from a one-sided love affair, makes very much the same observation, if more blithely. This takes a

swipe at dull, unimaginative, unpoetical academics
who try to rationalise such mysterious wonders as the
stars:

> For many thousand ages
> The steadfast stars above
> Have gazed upon each other
> With ever mournful love.
>
> They speak a certain language,
> So beautiful, so grand,
> Which none of the philologians
> Could ever understand.
>
> But I have learned it, learned it,
> For ever, by the grace
> Of studying one grammar,
> My heart's own darling's face.[15]

Such is the power of shared sympathies that,
according to Norman Marlow,[16] Housman's poem, 'Sin-
ners Rue' was originally subtitled 'After Heine'; its first
two stanzas are very close to being a straight translation
of no. LXII of Heine's 'Lyrisches Intermezzo':

> I walked alone and thinking,
> And faint the nightwind blew
> And stirred on mounds at crossways
> The flower of sinner's rue.
>
> Where the roads part they bury
> Him that his own hand slays,
> And so the weed of sorrow
> Springs at the four cross ways.

> (LP XXX)

Goethe considered the following lines of Marcus
Manilius, whose *Astronomica* Housman spend thirty
years painstakingly emending, to be magnificent:[17]

Who could know heaven save by heaven's gift and discover God save one who shares himself in the divine? Who could discern and compass in his narrow mind the vastness of this vaulted infinite, the dances of the stars, the blazing dome of heaven, and the planets' everlasting war against the signs, had not nature endowed our minds with divine vision, had turned to herself a kindred intelligence, and had prescribed so great a science? Who, unless there came from heaven a power which calls us heavenward to the sacred fellowship of nature?[18]

Lines like these recur too rarely in Manilius, but are nevertheless exciting when they come. Housman, labouring through the Roman's zodiacal erudition can, as poet, but feebly rejoin:

> And since, my soul, we cannot fly
> To Saturn nor to Mercury,
> Keep we must, if keep we can,
> These foreign laws of God and man.
>
> (LP XII)

There we have it: a scholar-poet invoking the divine to appear in an age when earthly, and starry, gods held sway, and, nearly two thousand years later, a scholar-poet living in an age of Christianity grudging the existence of a single divine being. To Arnold, however, religion was in the highest art (say of Michelangelo) – and vice versa – whether it was invoking or revoking the divine.

The next poem from which I quote the last three verses was tentatively begun in February 1896, a month before *A Shropshire Lad* was published, and finished in April 1922 only six months before *Last Poems* came out. In other words, although it was the product of two periods of Housman's poetical 'excitement', the Great War – and 750,000 young British soldiers – had, in just four years in between these periods, been and gone 'to eternity' in a patriotic effort that must have put the ethos of 'doing one's duty' under his closest scrutiny:

Iniquity it is; but pass the can.[19]
My lad, no pair of kings our mothers bore;
Our only portion is the estate of man:
We want the moon, but we shall get no more.

If here to-day the cloud of thunder lours
To-morrow it will hie on far behests;
The flesh will grieve on other bones than ours
Soon, and the soul will mourn in other breasts.

The troubles of our proud and angry dust
Are from eternity, and shall not fail.
Bear them we can, and if we can we must.
Shoulder the sky, my lad, and drink your ale.

(LP IX)

Housman never espoused massive memorials, pouring out his soulful or doleful thoughts; he worked on a small scale as the part-time poet he was. Primarily he was an academic, and the very simplicity of the rhythmical quatrains he favoured served to restrain him from writing epics. Yet he steals into our unconscious, and can suddenly grip us. Milton wrote over 9,000 lines in *Paradise Lost* 'to justify the ways of God to man', whereas Housman – a beer drinker who published a little over 2,000 lines in a long lifetime – was even equal to making an immortal joke out of it:

And malt does more than Milton can
To justify God's ways to man.

(ASL LXII)

HOUSMAN AND THE PERSIAN

Ah, my Belovéd, fill the Cup that clears
TO-DAY of past Regrets and future Fears –
To-morrow? – Why, Tomorrow I may be
Myself with Yesterday's Sev'n Thousand Years.[20]

Khayyám is an attractive drinking companion. Housman too, was fond of food and drink: 'The man who has never been half-drunk is a stranger to generous emotion',[21] he decreed. There is much drinking in the *Rubáiyát of Omar Khayyám* in defiance of philosophers and physicians:

The Grape that can with Logic absolute
The Two-and-Seventy jarring Sects confute:
The sovereign Alchemist that in a trice
Life's leaden metal into Gold transmute:

The mighty Mahmud, Allah-breathing Lord,
That all the misbelieving and black Horde
Of Fears and Sorrows that infest the Soul
Scatters before him with his whirlwind Sword.

And that inverted Bowl we call The Sky,
Whereunder crawling coop'd we live and die,
Lift not your hands to *It* for help – for It
As impotently rolls as you as I.[22]

So far from being indignant at the indifference of nature he is wise to it and accepts his vulnerability.

Content you with the mimic heaven
And on the earth remain

echoed Housman. Also, in a more sombre tone, he thought:

111

> For nature, heartless, witless nature,
> Will neither care nor know
> What stranger's feet may find the meadow
> And trespass there and go,
> Nor ask amid the dews of morning
> If they are mine or no.
>
> (LP XL)

Omar Khayyám, as rendered in Fitzgerald in lines every bit as beautiful as Housman's, expresses the firm hope that he will be remembered. He urges:

> And when Yourself with silver Foot shall pass
> Among the Guests Star-scatter'd on the Grass,
> And in your joyous errand reach the spot
> Where I made One–turn down an empty Glass![23]

Drink is the great anaesthetiser while 'the feather pate of folly/Bears the falling sky':

> Oh, 'tis jesting, dancing, drinking
> Spins the heavy world around.
> If young hearts were not so clever,
> Oh, they would be young for ever:
> Think no more; 'tis only thinking
> Lays lads underground.
>
> (ASL XLIX)

When Housman felt most like dying – at the time of Moses' presumable rejection of his love – he busied himself in study not in 'jesting, dancing, drinking'. However, the point of the poem above is to advocate distraction from sad thoughts. 'Come fill the Cup', the Persian keeps saying; he never becomes maudlin in his meandrine musings. He wants to remain practical as

well as philosophical and not, like Housman, grumb-
ling around the graveside. But Housman, who loved
wild flowers and blossom, had his own wistful form of
common sense:

> – Ah, life, what is it but a flower?
> Why must true lovers sigh?
> Be kind, have pity, my own, my pretty, –
> 'Good-bye, young man, good-bye.'
>
> (ASL V)

This again is reminiscent of Omar Khayyám:

> Oh, come with old Khayyám, and leave the Wise
> To talk; one thing is certain, that Life flies;
> One thing is certain, and the Rest is Lies;
> The Flower that once has blown for ever dies.[24]

'The Wise' refers to those Sufi theologians who became
obsessively preoccupied with the threat of Hell, and the
prospect of Paradise, to the extent of losing sight of how
to live in the present, as a direct result of their elaborate
system of divination loosely termed 'Mysticism'. The
above idea was thus expressed in the Book of Job:

> Man that is born of woman is of few days, and full of
> trouble. He cometh forth like a flower, and is cut
> down: he fleeth also as a shadow, and continueth
> not.[25]

The Book of Ecclesiastes, which seems to have exerted
such a powerful influence on Housman, had the following, almost hedonistic, recipe for dealing with life:

> And I turned myself to behold wisdom, and mad-
> ness, and folly: for what can the man do that cometh

after the king? even that which hath already been done.[26]

And concludes; perhaps allowing us a moderate 'tipple':

There is nothing better for a man, than that he should eat and drink, and that he should make his soul enjoy good in his labour. This also I saw, that it was from the hand of God.[27]

Perhaps neither Khayyám nor Housman would say grace before meals unless by refraining they would offend against the proprieties.

Although Housman was aware also of the bad sides of life, he described himself as a Cyrenaic; 'I am not a pessimist but a pejorist ... I respect the Epicureans more than the Stoics', he wrote.[28] By inventing the word 'pejorist' Housman meant to show the useful, practical side of his pessimism. It took Job to shout out 'Alleluia!' when abandoned by all. In spite of his afflictions Job ascribes no wrong to God, but Housman, his thoughts on soldiers, did so in LP XXXVII;

What God abandoned, these defended,
And saved the sum of things for pay.

When his youngest brother Herbert was killed, Housman alluded in 'Astronomy' to a well-known star being 'sunk underground', whereas when 'old Khayyám' anticipates his death he knows that life will go on though the 'Moon of Heav'n' will shine on him but once:

Ah, Moon of my Delight who know'st me wane,
The Moon of Heav'n is rising once again:
How oft hereafter rising shall she look
Through this same Garden after me – in vain![29]

A famous mathematician in his day, Omar Khayyám was highly proficient in astronomy and was the author of some astronomical tables.[30] Here he forges an analogy with the toy known as Farrusi Khiyal, a magic lantern affair still to be found in India:

> For in and out, above, about, below,
> 'Tis nothing but a Magic Shadow-show,
> Play'd in a Box whose Candle is the Sun,
> Round which we Phantom Figures come and go.[31]

Khayyám was referring to a silhouette toy theatre, with which to entertain children, but it is also possible that he thought in terms of 'revolutions', that the Earth might revolve around the Sun, even though he was born just after the Battle of Hastings, nearly five centuries before Copernicus's treatise.

At the end of his introduction to the Third Edition of the Rubaiyát in 1868 Fitzgerald wrote:

> Readers may be content to believe with me, that, while the wine Omar celebrates is simply Juice of the Grape, he bragged more than he drank of it, in very defiance of that Spiritual Wine which left its Votaries sunk in Hypocrisy or Disgust.

Terence's wanderings in Shropshire and London as the Shropshire lad were, although emotionally controlled, an exemplar of all young lads' journeyings through the ordeals of first love, of first leaving home, and of first reactions to the city. His reactions to death, however, became the focal point of his poems as he moped in the pub 'melancholy mad', quaffing deeply the while (ASL LXII). Khayyám chose a tavern table as the setting for a debate about the meaning of mankind's existence and all that this can provoke. He employed the grape, the cup, the tavern itself (the Temple) and so on, as emblems in an attack on the spurious and decadent Sufism of his day, offering as alternative – as Housman did – some guidance on how to face the sorrows of life and the mysteries of death. Housman, however, was in truth a stoic rather than a Cyrenaic; Khayyám was, in the guise accorded to him by Fitzgerald, an Epicurean.

The *Rubáiyát*, translated by Fitzgerald and published on 9 April 1859 (two weeks after Housman's birth), had by the 1890s become one of the most popular books of poetry. Ten years later, *A Shropshire Lad* was a best-seller alongside it. Both books were published in editions of every shape and size, the most attractive having embossed and inlaid covers; both were also published in pocket-sized editions. Although Housman never once mentions the Persian in published letter or lecture, he would undoubtedly have read him and commiserated with him over the evanescence of life. *A Shropshire Lad* contains sixty-three short poems which, like the quatrains of the *Rubáiyát*, are strung together without benefit of a narrative thread, relying instead on their author's or translator's judicious arrangement of the verses. Thus, in both books, there is a fleeting illusion of a long, coherent poem. Compare the following verses in each; first, from Khayyám:

> AWAKE! for Morning in the Bowl of Night
> Has flung the Stone that puts the Stars to Flight:
> And Lo! the Hunter of the East has caught
> The Sultán's Turret in a Noose of light.[32]

Housman also is cheerful on rising, even if he has become gloomy by evening:

> Wake: the silver dusk returning
> Up the beach of darkness brims,

'FALLING' STREAM

LUDLOW, from the south

'LABOURING' HIGHWAY

'STANDING' HILL

And the ship of sunrise burning
Strands upon the eastern rims.

Wake: the vaulted shadow shatters
Trampled to the floor it spanned,
And the tent of night in tatters
Straws the sky-pavilioned land.

(ASL IV)

Compared with the hymn 'Awake my soul, and with
the sun / Thy daily stage of duty run'[33], Housman is, in
the following stanzas, similarly buoyant. The difference
is that Housman paints a wonderfully well-observed
sunrise. 'Straws the sky-pavilioned land' might remind
one that Khayyám was by origin a tent-maker,
'Khayyám' in fact signifying 'tentmaker':

Khayyám, who stitched the tents of science,
Has fallen in grief's furnace and been suddenly burned;
The shears of Fate have cut the tent ropes of his life,
And the broker of Hope has sold him for nothing![34]

However I find Housman's sunrise at the start of
his convoluted, mighty 'Revolution' (LP XXXVI) somewhat too clouded over with 'Pre-Raphaelite' metaphors:

West and away the wheels of darkness roll,
Day's beamy banner up the east is borne,
Spectres and fears, the nightmare and her foal,
Drown in the golden deluge of the morn.

The start of 'God's Acre' (AP XI) strides forward, simply
and effectively until the syllables expand into an easy
rhythm. Indeed this would stand as a short, precise
quatrain in its own right, although this is the start of
twenty-two unbroken lines of poetry:

> Morning up the eastern stair
> Marches, azuring the air,
> And the foot of twilight still
> Is stolen toward the western sill.

More characteristically, Housman's other 'early start' refers allegorically to the dead who march no more:

> Wake not for the world-heard thunder
> Nor the chime that earthquakes toll.
>
> (LP XXIX)

In 'The Welsh Marches' sunrise is likened to a flag, and sunset to bleeding, in a clever mixture of description and allusion:

> The flag of morn in conqueror's state
> Enters at the English Gate:
> The vanquished eve, as night prevails,
> Bleeds upon the road to Wales.
>
> (ASL XXVIII)

Housman's rhetoric sometimes seems a little gauche compared with Khayyám's. He must have been amazed by the enthusiastic reception so many thousands gave to such a personal book as *A Shropshire Lad*. But Persian poets were aware that their poems' meanings were what their readers read into them and, realising this, Fitzgerald used a remarkably free hand in his translation. As the *Rubáiyát* was, in a sense, transformed both by Fitzgerald and by each reader's response to its many ambiguities, so the poems in *A Shropshire Lad*, originally engendered by Housman's personal 'inner conflicts', were transformed by their cumulative strength and their ability to say different things to readers both at the turn of the century and today.

NOTES

1. Hardy, 'An August Midnight'.
2. ASL XXIX.
3. Introduction to *Tess of the D'Urbervilles* (Penguin, 1978).
4. Hardy received an Honorary Degree from Jesus College in June 1913: that was the occasion of their meeting.
5. Letter to M. Pollet, 5.2.33.
6. Letter to Houston Martin, 27.9.35. M/S H. Martin. *A.E.H.*, p. 198. *Letters*, p. 376.
7. Hardy, 'The Darkling Thrush'; also Arnold's 'darkling plain' from 'Dover Beach'. Edward Thomas's 'Adlestrop' has 'all the birds / Of Oxfordshire and Gloucestershire'.
8. Written by Housman on the flyleaf of a copy of Manilius I which he gave to Walter Headlam.
9. cf 'The stars have not dealt me the worst they can do' (AP XVII).
10. In *Far from the Madding Crowd*.
11. Theocritus, Idyll XIII ('Hylas'), trans. C. S. Calverley.
12. Job, ch. 38, v. 31.
13. No. 81 of the *Rubáiyát of Omar Khayyám*, trans. E. Fitzgerald (1st edn 1859; 2nd edn 1868; 3rd edn 1872; 4th edn 1879; 5th edn 1889; all quotes are from Collins, 1953 which includes 1st, 2nd and 5th edns).
14. Leslie Stephen Lecture, 1933. The primeval note, here, would appeal to Ted Hughes.
15. Heine, *Es stehen unbeweglich*, trans. James Thompson (Cassell, 1929); Thompson invented 'philolog*ians*'.
16. Norman Marlow, *A.E. Housman, Scholar and Poet* (Routledge & Kegan Paul, 1958).
17. Goethe knew the first sentence by heart and wrote it in the visitors' book at the summit of the Brocken on 4 September 1748.
18. Manilius, *Astronomica*, Book 2, lines 115–27 trans. G. P. Goold (Loeb Classical Library, Heinemann, 1977); '. . . the signs' mean 'of the Zodiac'.

19. Cf. Tennyson's:

> Fill the can, and fill the cup:
> All the windy ways of men
> Are by dust that rises up,
> And is lightly laid again.
>
> *The Vision of Sin* IV, xviii

'Can' was then a common word for jug.

20. *Rubáiyát*, no. 20. 1st edn.
21. From some sentences in a Notebook held by Trinity College, Cambridge library. Published in R. P. Graves's *A. E. Housman: The Scholar-Poet* (Routledge & Kegan Paul, 1979).
22. *Rubáiyát*, nos 61, 62 and 78, 2nd edn.
23. Ibid., no. 110, 2nd edn.
24. Ibid., no. 26, 1st edn.
25. Job, ch. 14, v. 1 and 2.
26. Ecclesiastes, ch. 2. v. 12.
27. Ibid., v. 24.
28. Letter to Pollet, 5.2.33.
29. *Rubáiyát*, no. 74, 1st edn.
30. Entitled Ziji-Maliksháhá.
31. *Rubáiyát*, no. 46, 1st edn.
32. Ibid., no. 1, 1st edn.
33. Words by Bishop T. Ken (1637–1711) for 'Morning Hymn'. Ken was a writer of devotional prose and verse.
34. Quoted by Fitzgerald in his Introduction to 1st edn, but not included in the book of poems.

5 · SHROPSHIRE: THE NAMING OF ARCADIA

O Singer of Persephone!
In the dim meadows desolate
Dost thou remember Sicily?

Oscar Wilde, *Theocritus*

I am of Shropshire, my shines be sharpe;
Ley wode to the fyre, and dress me my harpe.

(Anon.)

In Chapter 1, examples are given of countryside which might have been labelled Arcadian: the Lasithi Plain, the Vale of Tempe, Arkhadia itself, and one of the reputed locations for the Garden of Eden, namely the plain around Babylon about sixty miles south of modern Baghdad. Ironically, by AD 730, Baghdad had become a city fabled for its learning under the auspices of the new Islamic religion. In Britain, Borrowdale in the Lake District, or the Wye and Golden Valleys in Herefordshire, or the Clun Valley in Shropshire may still be viewed (if one ignores recent building such as new factories in the Golden Valley) as modern Arcadias.

Milton picked out four candidates for the Garden of Eden: the 'fair field of Enna' in the heart of Sicily, the town being surrounded by dramatic hills within which, a myth tells us, was to be found a grove in which it was eternally spring; 'Daphne by Orontes' – another famous grove, situated near the river Orontes (near Assi), five miles south of Antioch (now Antakya in Turkey); 'the Nyseian Isle' – a beautiful but untraceable island, also the name both of a nymph and of a mountain upon which Dionysus is said to have invented wine. Finally there was 'under the Ethiop line / By Nilus' head' – at the head of the Nile and near the equator, perhaps somewhere in the Sudan. I suspect that Nysa is one of the fabled Islands of the Blessed,[1] but all the other places are real enough. Milton picked the highest available vantage-point on which to perch Satan – namely the Tree of Life – from which to scan all of Eden, yet Satan could glimpse no 'real' place as lovely as the Garden. As Kipling put it, 'But the Glory of the Garden lies in more than meets the eye.'

Shakespeare's Arcadian island on which the ship was wrecked in *The Tempest* is thought to have been inspired by the tiny, and, in his day, still very remote, island of Bermuda; he needed to evoke an hallucinatory atmosphere in balmy conditions for a play which drew its power from its magical fairy-tale quality. Hardy used the Wessex landscape to give vitality and depth to his characters as they moved across its surface; Robert Louis Stevenson loved the Lothians; Wordsworth was enraptured by Cumberland; for Scott it was the Borders;[2] and Kipling had a soft spot for Sussex; while Herrick had to make do with Dartmoor which he considered detestably damp. It was the 'spirit' of these places which these poets caught, not lavishly detailed geographical descriptions. Housman was both clever and possibly lucky to choose Shropshire. Not only is it still today, for the main part, very beautiful but, being next to Wales and having experienced so much border intercourse, possesses unique qualities. Hilaire Belloc knew his history and described the men that 'see the Severn strong' as having '. . . the secret of the rocks / And the oldest kind of song'.

Sometimes there were already spirits in the hills. The Eildon Hills in Roxburghshire, for example, were

the subject of much legend of Evil Ones and Fairy
Queens. As for Housman's South Shropshire, even fifty
years ago the Clee Hills might have been described as
being inhabited by earth spirits. It was the haunt of
'witches' and much folklore. Housman remained a poet
of the earth who looked now and then to the stars of
heaven, if not the Heaven of the Blessed, for comfort
and hope. His 'lads' seem to have their feet on the earth
and their hands busy scratching out comfortable graves
for themselves. While Milton's Adam was free to
choose his destiny, the Shropshire lad, in Housman's
alternative vision of a lost paradise, is helpless against
the uncaring hand of fate:

> 'Tis a long way further than Knighton,
> A quieter place than Clun,
> Where doomsday may thunder and lighten
> And little 'twill matter to one.

> (ASL L)

Like beauty, which is in the eye of the beholder,
Arcadia is, more than ever, all in the imagination of one's
mind. The French author, Alain-Fournier, chiefly remembered for his nostalgic novel, *Le Grand Meaulnes*,
sought to evoke, with the help of lovely unspoilt countryside, the less lovely mysteries, the idealisms, the
longings and the eternal frustrations of adolescents.
Housman, too, summoned up a 'lost domain' that had
as its basis a real region that he called the 'land of lost
content'. It had to have beauty, as suffering lads would
have no leisure, in the face of stinging sleet or dren-
ching rain, to reflect on any other awful predicament
but set about finding shelter where they can dry themselves off. They need to be able to wander at will,
however mournfully, in such clement weather that the
very trees seem to whisper advice to them. They need

to have beautiful hills, towards which to lift their sad eyes so that, as they take their leave, it is the familiar 'blue remembered hills' that tug at their heartstrings. ASL XXXVII describes such a departure into reminiscence:

> Low in the forsaken west
> Sank the high-reared head of Clee . . .

Most of us can match this kind of feeling as we leave, say, some island, leaning over the ship's rail and watching the silhouettes of mountain-tops gradually diminish, until they sink from view. The slowness of a boat seems to enhance any inclination for melancholia. Even if the holiday was a disappointing one, the memories evoked by the skyline seem to act like magic on the tender, sentimental core of our being. Finally, back at home, we may recall:

> Into my heart an air that kills
> From yon far country blows:
> What are those blue remembered hills,
> What spires, what farms are those?

Closing our eyes, we conjure up the memory:

> That is the land of lost content,
> I see it shining plain,
> The happy highways where I went
> And cannot come again.
>
> (ASL XL)

Into eight lines Housman has condensed nostalgia.

H. V. Morton, in his amusing, informative *In Search of England*, explained his motive for writing it after a safe return to London from the Middle East. It had been bad enough being an exile, but when in addition he was very ill his sense of nostalgia had been goaded beyond endurance:

> In the black depths of misery, I climbed a hill over-looking Jerusalem, unaffected by the fact that this has been considered the best of all places to die, and, turning as accurately as I could in the direction of England, I gave way to a wave of homesickness that almost shames me now when I recollect it. I find it impossible in cold blood, and at this distance, to put into words the longings that shook me. I have forgotten the pain in the neck but I shall never forget the pain in the heart.[3]

Is Shropshire really worth crying over? Do we, for instance, really miss familiar outlines of hills? This is from ASL XLI, and re-affirms a basic human need:

> In my own shire, if I was sad,
> Homely comforters I had:
> The earth, because my heart was sore,
> Sorrowed for the son she bore;
> And standing hills, long to remain,
> Shared their short-lived comrade's pain.

Whereas this poem contains a list of the beauties of the palliating flora – the 'purple crocus pale', 'lady-smocks' and 'bluebells in the azured wood', the previous poem of 'lost content' describes, very broadly, the main characteristics of farmland Shropshire. Certainly the hills can look blue, and I have observed the Wrekin and Clee hills assume an appearance of purest cobalt blue on late summer afternoons. 'Hell Gate' and 'Heaven Gate', with the second appropriately nearer the summit, are points on the path up the Wrekin's most used north-facing ascent. (One doubts whether it was this 'Hell Gate' that Housman had in mind when he thus entitled his poem LP XXXI.) Four-fifths of the county is under cultivation and the rest is either rough hill pasture, as on the Long Mynd, or is built on. So Housman was right to ask about all those farms. However, he made the well-known blunder of donating a steeple to Hughley church:

> The vane on Hughley steeple
> Veers bright, a far-known sign . . .
>
> (ASL LXI)

Hughley's squat Elizabethan tower only sports a weathercock. Shrewsbury, on the other hand, has half a dozen spires, which Housman sketches accurately:

> High the vanes of Shrewsbury gleam
> Islanded in Severn stream;
> The bridges from the steepled crest
> Cross the water east and west.
>
> (ASL XXVIII)

By way of extenuation for making a mistake about a steeple, Housman confirmed: 'I was born in Worcestershire, not Shropshire, where I have never spent much time.'[4] Laurence compares the difference between the first draft, and the much improved second, of the following verse from 'The Merry Guide' (ASL XLII), a particularly 'pure' and untroubled Arcadian poem, to prove his point that Housman's poetry was best when 'subjected to much correction':[5]

(1st version)   By windy shires of woodland
                          With steeples dim-revealed,
                          And cloudy shadows racing
                          On all the endless weald.

(2nd version)   By blowing realms of woodland
With sunstruck vanes afield
And cloud-led shadows sailing
About the windy weald.

(ASL XLII)

The wind of nostalgia that 'killed' a few poems back is a virulent spirit with Housman, and those 'happy high-ways' could be walkers' tracks like the old monks' route, the 'Portway' on the backbone of the Long Mynd. Housman visited the place where his imagination did so much roaming only in order to gather some 'local colour', as he put it. He visited the county but twice, I believe, which is singular for a 'walking man'. (He climbed the Puy de Parioux – a mountain of about 3,500 feet in the Massif Central – at the age of seventy.) As a young man he far preferred to take a holiday visiting his friends the Wises at Woodchester, on the wooded western edge of the Cotswolds, or to visit the Continent, a fixed annual habit from middle age onwards. His wanderings in Shropshire were thus almost entirely poetic ones. By imagining it one cannot lose one's dreams of Arcady.

We know why he chose Shropshire. It was because from 'Mount Pisgah' he had ruminated on the distant, western skyline where 'sank the high-reared head of Clee'. He had lived within his large, close-knit family at Fockbury near Bromsgrove between the ages of fourteen and eighteen and a half. Had he lived at this impressionable age at, say, Morpeth then it might have been a 'Northumberland lad' that, in the course of time, had yearned for his Cheviots; if at Clitheroe in Lancashire, it might have been the deep brown bulk of Pendle Hill, so steeped in local sentiment, that was the focus for such special reverie. From west to east, Bodmin Moor, Dartmoor, Exmoor, the Quantocks, the Mendips, the Cotswolds and so on, are areas every one of which is now designated as having 'outstanding natural beauty'. Some, especially in the north, have besides been earmarked as National Parks, and while the Shropshire hill country is not one of these, it is officially termed 'outstandingly beautiful', and parts of it have been acquired by the National Trust. Housman explained:

> I had a sentimental feeling for Shropshire because its hills were our western horizon. I know Ludlow and Wenlock, but my topographical details – Hughley, Abdon under Clee – are sometimes quite wrong. Remember that Tyrtaeus was not a Spartan.[6]

Housman was a Worcestershire lad but has been adopted by Shropshire as their poet; Tyrtaeus was in the seventh century BC Sparta's national poet, although probably in fact an Athenian. Regarding 'topographical details', 'Bredon Hill' (ASL XXI), written about five years before publication of *A Shropshire Lad*, is the earliest poem destined for that book in which a particular place is named. Since his boyhood, Housman would have been familiar with Bredon Hill because it is about twenty miles from both Bromsgrove and Woodchester, midway between them in a direct north-south line. The poem speaks of all the bells ringing in the 'coloured counties' – a phrase which took some time to invent – around Bredon Hill, which indeed they do to this day. Within about two miles from the summit there are a dozen little village churches – though not steepled, as Housman suggests, in 'steeples far and near' – which encircle this isolated and, to some minds, prepossessing hillock.

Breidden Hill, pronounced as in Bredon, while it has far fewer churches in its vicinity, might easily have been drafted into *A Shropshire Lad* had Housman so wished. (The Severn flows within a few miles of both hills!) It is an elevation every bit as high as the Wrekin and which, only a mile into Powys, has a long clear view over the border to Shrewsbury and beyond. It also has some historical importance, being one of the three possible sites for Caractacus's last battle against the Romans – a fact Housman could well have used in a poem. Bredon Hill is a good forty miles south of the Shropshire border. As Housman was talking in a general way about bells ringing in countryside, Breidden would have suited his purpose. Obviously *after* publication the 'perpetual tinkering'[7] in which Wordsworth indulged did not interest Housman, yet 'Tis time, I think, by Wenlock town' (ASL XXXIX) had for him, then, the more local 'Stourbridge town' in the first draft, written at the same time as the Bredon poem. The greatest number of place-names is in XXXVII (in which the 'high-reared head of Clee' is seen), a *tour de force* of nostalgic evocation; here again we imagine 'standing hills':

> And if my foot returns no more
> To Teme nor Corve nor Severn shore,
> Luck, my lads, be with you still
> By falling stream and standing hill,
> By chiming tower and whispering tree,
> Men that made a man of me.

Housman must have nurtured strong feelings for the southern part of Shropshire, because, in the north wall, beneath the charming (and continually chiming) tower – a 'far-known sign' – of St Lawrence's, the superb, imposing parish church of Ludlow, are incarcerated Housman's mortal remains. Against advice Sir Walter Scott had to insist vigorously on being buried in the old abbey ruins of Dryburgh because the countryside about had been dear to him. Ludlow is at the southern extremity of Shropshire, roughly in the middle of its southern border, so Housman's plaque, by being on the north-west wall, faces north towards Long Mynd and the smaller intervening hills around Craven Arms, a perspective that is entirely apposite.

The South Shropshire District Council recently produced a colourful little brochure under the title *Close Your Eyes and Think of England*. They wrote that south Shropshire

> has arguably the greatest variety of scenery from grouse moor to marshland found in any district of England. The quality too is exceptional. Over 80% of the area is in the Shropshire Hills Area of Outstanding Natural Beauty.

The hills are distinctive not only because of their mound shapes, steep-sided but smooth, but also for the individual peculiarity of the main ridges. There is some drama: Caer Caradoc, named after one of the bravest of the Welsh princes that fought against the Romans, rises dramatically from the narrow flat Church Stretton valley. From its top spectacular views can be seen, especially northwards, across the expanding Shrewsbury plain, closed to the east by the Wrekin rising in the distance like a pyramid – a shape emphasised particularly by a low morning or evening sun. Rising to its west from the Shrewsbury plain, but much closer, the huge less wooded bulk of the Long Mynd stretches due southwards parallel to Caer Caradoc for about ten miles.

If Housman had realised that the Long Mynd was made up of the most ancient rock[8] in Britain, he might have introduced the Long Mynd into *A Shropshire Lad*. Its long broad back, which men on horseback used to dislike crossing on winter evenings for fear of losing their way, is like that of a great beached whale. Except for some steep-sided intrusive valleys, called 'batches' by locals (e.g. Cardingmill Valley), which have been cleft, over time immemorial, by the erosion of water, it is smooth and featureless, polished by winds and rains and bleached by the sun. It is grazing land for sheep. At its eastern base runs the Church Stretton fault, as famed and as long as the Great Glen Fault which cuts across the top of Scotland from Inverness to Mull. 'High in the folded hill' (ASL XLII) is a perfect description of the view looking from either north or south from the central heights of the Long Mynd.

The surface of Wenlock Edge, formed of soft fossiliferous mudstone and limestone rich in marine fauna, is still wooded, which makes it difficult to obtain a clear view north to the plain in which Hughley church sits with its conical cap by way of a 'steeple'. Housman uses the scenery perfectly, as Wenlock Edge has wooded slopes – and again the wind is used as a restless, ageless force that can thresh its way through the leaves of trees and awaken nostalgia in hearts, time and time again:

On Wenlock Edge the wood's in trouble;
His forest fleece the Wrekin heaves;
The gale, it plies the saplings double,
And thick on Severn snow the leaves.

'Twould blow like this through holt and hanger
When Uricon the city stood:
'Tis the old wind in the old anger,
But then it threshed another wood.

(ASL XXXI)

This recalls, for me, Christ's analogy of the regenerated spirit:

Marvel not that I said unto thee, Ye must be born
again. The wind bloweth where it listeth, and thou
hearest the sound thereof, but canst not tell whence it
cometh, and whither it goeth: so is every one that is
born of the Spirit.[9]

For clear reasons of alliteration Uriconium has been
abbreviated; in any case it should strictly speaking be
Viroconium which indicates the origin of the name
'Wrekin'. However, 'holt and hanger' fit perfectly, 'hanger' being an old term, still with currency in some rural
areas, for a wood on a steep hillside; and 'holt' meaning
a small plantation of trees. The undulating plain from
Shrewsbury through Telford to the Staffordshire border
was once famed for its fifty square miles of forest, the
Worfe Forest, a former royal hunting ground.

'Hanger' was also a short, flat-sided sword with a
curved tip, a weapon similar to the Roman sword. This
is particularly fitting for the reference to Uriconium,
'The White Town in the Woodland', founded by the
14th Legion in AD 68 and which became a thriving
county town, larger even than Silchester. It must have
seemed like a copy in miniature of Rome, with its great
baths, town hall and temple. The Romans departed in
the early fifth century, and Uriconium – now Wroxeter –
was burnt to the ground by Saxons or Celts.

Upstream a few miles, Shrewsbury, then called
Pengwerne, became in the fifth and sixth centuries the
seat of the Kings of Powis until Offa took control of it in
779. Thereafter it became one of the chief cities of the
Saxon kings. After the Conquest the town, now under
the sway of the Earls of Shrewsbury, was repeatedly
attacked by the Welsh who, though often repulsed,
captured it in 1215. But they held it for only six years.
Edward I made it his headquarters during his two
campaigns against the Welsh. In 1283 David, the last

ADAM AND EVE IN PARADISE, from the painting by Jan 'Velvet'
Brueghel, 1599 (*Collection HM the Queen*)

THE WREKIN AT SUNSET

ruling Prince of Wales, was tried and condemned to death there. Thus, after the Romans had left in the early fifth century, the Celts of Shrewsbury held at bay Mercians and Danes, but had to capitulate to the Normans. As late as Henry VIII's reign, the English were still obliged to put up resistance against Celts there, which is why Housman chose Shrewsbury to personify mankind's eternal troubles. As he put it in 'The Welsh Marches':

> The flag of morn in conqueror's state
> Enters at the English gate:
> The vanquished eve, as night prevails,
> Bleeds upon the road to Wales.

The Severn would have run with blood in those days of border warfare, as Mercian fought off Dane to the east and Celt to the west. Correspondingly Housman paints a lurid picture:

> When Severn down to Buildwas ran
> Coloured with the death of man,
> Couched upon her brother's grave
> The Saxon got me on the slave.
>
> (ASL XXVIII)

The Normans rightly thought they would endure, since they could build such good castles. Their smallest castle, at Clun, placed almost as far west as any of the little Roman hill forts is now almost gone, such is its state of ruin. But Ludlow Castle, where for centuries men dined and slept with their swords ready to be drawn ringing from their scabbards, is the best preserved border stronghold. It was here that the capable Lord Wardens of the Marches lived, gazing with wary, suspicious eyes through the arrow slits in the direction of Wales. Whereas in England, swords had been hung up and had rusted in their sheaths, Ludlow swords were shining. Peace, when it eventually came to the town – notwithstanding a slight 'tiff' in the Civil War – brought with it fairs and fun and 'the handsome of face and handsome of heart':

> The lads in their hundreds to Ludlow come
> in for the fair,
> There's men from the barn and the forge and
> the mill and the fold,
> The lads for the girls and the lads for
> the liquor are there,
> And there with the rest are the lads that
> will never be old.
>
> (ASL XXIII)

When Housman speaks of fighting it is not so much to dwell on battles long ago as to relate them to the relentless onslaught of misfortune and doubt which buffets its way deep into men's hearts. So it was 'On Wenlock Edge' – and the tower he refers to here is of church not castle:

> Come you home a hero,
> Or come not home at all,
> The lads you leave will mind you
> Till Ludlow tower shall fall.
>
> (ASL III)

It is like passing under a border watchtower as one leaves Ludlow, in the south-eastern corner of Shropshire, for Worcestershire, because Titterstone Clee has a distinctively sharp-edged profile. Though not as high, its gable-end is easily distinguished from the twin

134

mound-shaped summits of Brown Clee adjoining it to the north. Even if seen from the heights of Bromsgrove, twenty-five miles directly westwards, the silhouette of that 'watchtower' is recognisable. There used to be coal mining on both Titterstone and Brown Clee hills and, since basalt (dhustone) is found on Titterstone, there are now extensive roadstone quarries despoiling the leeward, east-facing slope. Fortunately no-one can despoil its noble outline, even as seen from the Midlands. Again:

> Low in the forsaken west
> Sank the high-reared head of Clee, . . .
>
> (ASL XXXVII)

The small hills that beset the banks of such modest rivers as the Clun, West and East Onny and Corve in south Shropshire must have given welcome protection, due to their slopes being graced with 'hangers', to the earliest Salopians seeking refuge from Celtic terrorists. They now seem to have become the haven for a great deal of the invading coniferous woodland. It is not as sleepy as it looks, however, and since Housman in light-hearted vein was fond of quoting Swift's disdainful remark to the effect that 'the bulk of mankind is as qualified for flying as for thinking', he might well have been taken aback to discover that most 'villagers' in the Clun Valley have heard of him. Indeed, when a young Shropshire lad[10] was killed in the Falklands War in 1982, it was a cherry tree that was planted in his memory, outside the church porch of Clungunford. This is an acknowledgement of Housman's concern for young soldiers, an interest that led him, for example, to write to the Dean of Lincoln to take issue with the Dean's advocacy of sexual abstinence for soldiers during the Great War!

This stanza conveys both the somniferous quality of the air, and also the deeper malaise which comes with responsibilities which mankind will always rise to meet. Compare this with 'Far I hear the bugle blow' (ASL LVI):

> On the idle hill of summer,
> Sleepy with the flow of streams,
> Far I hear the steady drummer
> Drumming like a noise in dreams.
>
> (ASL XXXV)

The poem ends with a stirring last line, reminiscent of 'man that was born of woman' and 'rise up: take up thy bed and walk'. It is also worth remarking that the poem finishes on an anapaest built from three monosyllables, 'I will rise', after three and a half lines of evenly flowing trochaics that include every open vowel sound. This ensures that the ending, enunciated in a determined voice, or even in a resigned one, is quite distinct, almost like a voice answering a cry that has echoed down the ages:

> Far the calling bugles hollo,
> High the screaming fife replies,
> Gay the files of scarlet follow:
> Woman bore me, I will rise.

The popular early-Victorian Irish novelist and songwriter Samuel Lover astutely remarked: 'To awaken sympathy by the simplest words will go farther in a song than pomp of language and elaborate polish.' The seemingly simple poem is skilfully composed, and this last verse is potent and suggestive. Burns and Lover and Belloc[11] would each have liked this ditty used by Housman which is so like the triolet from Mary Webb's 'Love in Idleness' which begins:

> Under the sun
> There's nothing new
> Poem or pun
> Under the sun.

Now Housman:

> Clunton and Clunbury,
> Clungunford and Clun,
> Are the quiestest places
> Under the sun.
>
> (ASL L)

It is a moot point whether Housman altered it to the 'quietest' from 'drunkenest', or whether he discovered the verse in its more genteel form.[12] There was once a malt house – part of it still stands – in Clun, but the epithet 'quietest' seems more suitable for the gentle mood that pervades the poem which follows the prefatory ditty:

> In valleys of springs of rivers,
> by Ony[13] and Teme and Clun,
> The country for easy livers,
> The quietest under the sun . . .

When some time ago I bought an early edition of *A Shropshire Lad* I found pressed between its pages a series of cuttings from the *Liverpool Post* and *Daily Post* of 1925, being responses to an article on 'Housman's Shropshire' which had also been slipped in among the other cuttings. One letter from a Lloyd Rawlings of Liverpool reads as follows:

Sir,

You have already allowed one correction to the interesting article in the 'Daily Post' on 'Housman's Shropshire', namely that the jingle on Clunbury, Clunton, Clungunford and Clun was not written by A.E. Housman. May I suggest a correction to the rhyme itself? As handed down for generations in my mother's family (well known in Clun), it stood . . . *(and here Mr Rawlings quotes the rhyme with 'drunkenest places'. He finishes:)* Perhaps there were two versions, the quiet ones insisting on the word 'drunkenest' and the drunken ones insisting on the word 'quietest'.

Today there are no more Rawlings in Clun or immediately surrounding district, but I did discover at Clun Post Office (once run by a Mr Rawlings) that the rhyme in question is still well-known in both forms.

Sedentary people on the boundary between two robust cultures will often be found to adopt characteristics from each, thus exhibiting a mixture of traits. Shropshire's hill country and those living there have a Welsh quality. Although it would be a mistake to speculate if this quality, detectable though it is in Housman's poetry, had anything to do with Celtic emotions, when talking about the 'inner nature of the proud Salopian' in relation to Housman's poetry, Edmund Vale has a theory:

This gaiety and sadness going hand in hand is in the people and in the scenery. You feel it by the Wrekin and on the Clee Hills. But it is an emanation that comes from the west and not from the east, from Radnor Forest, the Kerry Hills and the Berwyn Mountains.[14]

One has to read every poem in *A Shropshire Lad* to find one cheerful ending – and that is in the cynical XVIII. Two examples, XXXIX ('Tis time, I think, by Wenlock town' (or even II) 'Loveliest of trees, the cherry now'), gives rein to a sort of morbid, reflective Celtic spirit, while the Clun poem (L) is the worst of all in this respect. For, having begun with an introductory jingle and a description of truly perfect pastoral scenery, the bathetic ending is not, as in XXXV, a call to rise up and risk one's life for one's country. It is the voice of Death itself:

> 'Tis a long way further than Knighton,
> A quieter place than Clun,
> Where doomsday may thunder and lighten
> And little 'twill matter to one.
>
> (ASL L)

Knighton has been appropriated by Powys, which itself appropriated Radnorshire, though it actually sits on the border and shares scenery similar to Shropshire as it looks east to Ludlow down the Teme. Housman's grandfather on his mother's side, the Reverend John Williams, was, as well as being a competent classicist, something of a poet; his mother had inherited the latter trait and employed it in short lampoons about people she knew. But the fact that her father was of West Country extraction would be too easy an explanation for the passionate woes which were to be aroused in Housman. Indeed, the poet himself dismissed such speculation in one of the observations which he recorded in the notorious little notebook which he kept in his top pocket: 'If an Irish baby cries when teething it is quoted as an instance of the Celtic melancholy.'

During the period immediately after the First World War, when *A Shropshire Lad* was still extremely popular, the novels of Mary Webb were also becoming widely known and loved. Robert Lynd said of her:

> If it is necessary to classify novelists . . . Mary Webb must be put in a class that contains writers so differ-ent as Emily Brontë and Thomas Hardy, for whom the earth is predominantly a mystery – haunted land-scape inhabited by mortals who suffer . . . It is not too much, indeed, to say that in her writings fiction becomes a branch of poetry – a flowering branch that will still give pleasure for many years to come.[15]

Today she is undergoing something of a revival, and such novels as *Gone to Earth* (1917) and *Precious Bane* (1924) are becoming increasingly familiar; in them the beauties of the central and northern parts of Shropshire are reflected. *The Spring of Joy* is her best known book of poems. This is an example of her oneness with nature and her yearning spirit, and seems to capture some-thing of the passionate spirit that burns so fiercely in Sappho's verses:

> My heart has blossomed meekly as the thorn;
> It has its dews, and daisies two or three.
> The heaven's quicken, green as April corn –
> And oh, my love! when will you come to me?

With sapphic urgency *Precious Bane* ends with the heroine saying: 'I've chosen my bit of Paradise. 'Tis on your heart my dear acquaintance!'

Webb and Housman were both solitary walkers but unlike Housman she did nothing in her poems to curb the imaginative energy of her passionate reaction to Arcadia. In the above extract she exudes a rapture for even the tiniest daisy. Housman did likewise but there was always more of an incisive edge to the way in which he proceeded to relate such joy to personal griefs and doubts. When he left Worcestershire, he knew that part of his life, his carefree childhood days, had gone; when she left Shropshire she was bitterly upset and, when her husband left her, she literally faded away. She died at the age of 46.

Housman's poetry was, as we know, extremely carefully constructed and considered. Whereas he was the Shropshire poet of passion for remembered times and future solace, Mary Webb was passionate, even ecstatic, for 'the actual'. Whereas he was a Pre-Raphaelite, she was an Impressionist. She had a more virile and lively imagination than Housman and, as Walter de la Mare wrote, 'could seize the momentary'[16] sight, sound or smell. The great difference between her and Housman was that she hardly thought nature malevolent: it was her very comfort and source of re-juvenation.

Though the flesh-and-blood 'lads' of south Shropshire seem sensible, cheerful chaps, the country air refreshing and the landscape delightful, after sampling the pages of *A Shropshire Lad* for the first time one might be forgiven for backing off Shropshire soil for fear of being infected by a communal state of depression. But let us be thankful that Housman chose Shropshire. A county of huge skies which wander over rolling hill and lush field, it can easily override Housman's unwhole-some plots and festering nostalgia. However, another professor who wrote poetry, Edmund Wilson, wrote of Heine:

Doleful though his accents may sometimes be, he always lets in air and light to the mind. But Housman is closed from the beginning. His world has no open-ing horizons; it is a prison that one can only endure.[17]

141

How can one read Housman's 'The Merry Guide' (ASL XLII) and feel imprisoned by it? Admittedly there is, as Wilson wrote, 'no role for creation in Housman's scheme of things'[18] as a poet. Such jaded views of a universe grown sterile may be seen most clearly in 'The Culprit' (LP XIV):[19]

> For so the game is ended
> That should not have begun.
> My father and my mother
> They had a likely son,
> And I have none.

For me, Housman's sketches of landscape call to mind colour photographs, the colours of which after many years in a damp room have faded to that sepia colour of which the Victorians were so fond of in family portraits and in which hardly the glimmer of a smile is allowed – by the photographer – to flicker across their stony faces. The sun may shine, the blossom may move in the breeze, birds may sing, vanes gleam or clouds scud across fields; but nothing raises Housman's spirits. Any colour in his cheeks quickly pales as the anguish seeps through.

Why are we born if suffering is to be our lot? The very first poem of *A Shropshire Lad* begins merrily enough:

> Look left, look right, the hills are bright.
> The dales are light between,
> Because 'tis fifty years to-night
> That God has saved the Queen.

This poem is to be seen in its true colours with its contrasts mellowed with sepia; blackest of blacks against purest whites are best for poems of blazing beacons. Even the beautiful images of beacons reflected

in water, and being lit in swift succession, as painted by
Aeschylus in *Agamemnon* two thousand years ago, are
as vivid today as when they were written. For Lord
Macaulay it was 1588 that served as touchstone for his
poem of beacons. One feels that this sight may easily
have been seen from 'Mount Pisgah' above Fockbury in
Worcestershire; the very lines themselves seem to
spring out like fireworks:

> All night from tower to tower they sprang, they
>   sprang from hill to hill;
> Till the proud peak unfurled the flag o'er
>   Darwin's rocky dales,
> Till the volcanoes flared to heaven the
>   stormy hills of Wales,
> Till twelve fair counties saw the blaze on
>   Malvern's lonely height,
> Till steamed in crimson on the wind the
>   Wrekin's crest of light. . . .[20]

For Housman beacons blaze not so much to celebrate,
but rather to perpetuate, the memory of dead soldiers.
In 'Sinner's Rue' (LP XXX) the dead, being suicides, are
buried on the verges of crossroads, just as criminals
used to be hanged and buried at such out-of-the-way
places years ago. The poet takes grim comfort that even
in his sadness he is more fortunate than the suicides.
Housman did have his brighter moments, however,
such as when he discovered at his feet the uplifting
sight of a flower's rebirth, even in such a harsh setting:

> 'Tis spring; come out to ramble
> The hilly brakes around,
> For under thorn and bramble
> About the hollow ground
> The primroses are found.
>
> (ASL XXIX)

Housman can make you feel the breeze on your face; it comes from the west and still smells sweet, or if it comes from the colder east it may warm the heart:

> The winds out of the west land blow,
>   My friends have breathed them there;
> Warm with the blood of lads I know
>   Comes east the sighing air.
>
>   (ASL XXXVIII)

Well before the time *Last Poems* had been made ready for the press, Housman had the wind turning itself inside out while 'sighing':

> The sigh that heaves the grasses
> Whence thou wilt never rise
> Is of the air that passes
> And knows not if it sighs.
>
>   (LP XXVII)

Housman was never prosaic about the wind; in the Shropshire poems, for instance, it was where 'voices . . . are sown'. Clearly this 'sighing' for a 'west land' did not arise out of a genuine affection for Shropshire, but in order to focus his nostalgia. 'Sighing' and 'crying', 'winds' and 'waters': they are drawn into his loosely selected, universal metaphors which serve to convey nostalgia. Here is Masefield on the charms of the west wind:

> It's a warm wind, the west wind, full of bird's cries;
> I never hear the west wind but tears are in my eyes.
> For it comes from the west lands, the old brown hills,
> And April's in the west wind, and daffodils.

Actual places – 'living' ones as opposed to ruins – can be

fatally 'specific' and smack of incongruity, thus becoming 'mortal' and unromantic, even if they had once stimulated romantic longings. Had Housman chosen Norfolk as the repository for his doomed Arcadian homesickness it is unlikely that he could have imbued the chill of its east wind with credible heartwarming feelings.

Robert Louis Stevenson, for the last four years of his life, found his Arcadia – which granted him an all-too-brief respite from his accustomed ill-health – in Samoa in the South Pacific. Within a few months of the Scotsman's death, Housman as an act of homage copied into 'R.L.S.' (AP XXII) the memorable ditty which Stevenson had written in the South of France exactly ten years before the apoplectic fit that struck him down in his South Seas Arcadia. It could have been Housman's own Requiem. Stevenson had been far from well in Hyères:

> Here he lies where he longed to be;
> Home is the sailor, home from sea,
> And the hunter home from the hill.

When Stevenson wrote the sentimental poem 'To S. R. Crockett' his mind's eye returned to his homeland:

> Be it granted me to behold you again in dying,
> Hills of home! and to hear again the call;
> Hear about the graves of the martyrs the peewees
>   crying,
> And hear no more at all.

That poem begins 'Blows the wind to-day . . .' and Housman, again responding to restless, nostalgic winds – 'In the windless night-time', and catching the sounds of strange sighs – 'Soft the poplars sigh', approaches the

145

end of *A Shropshire Lad* in a vein of nostalgia that is quite pitiable. This is reminiscent of Stevenson's 'hear no more at all' or Sappho's cryptic 'Alone':

> He hears: no more remembered
> In fields where I was known,
> Here I lie down in London
> And turn to rest alone.

(ASL LII)

NOTES

1. As mentioned in 'Harmodius and Aristogeiton', anonymous sixth-century Greek poem.
2. Scott called a valley near his Abbotsford estate 'Rhymers Glen'.
3. H.V. Morton, *In Search of England* (Methuen, 1927).
4. Letter to M. Pollet, 5.2.33.
5. L. Housman, *A.E.H.* (Cape, 1937), p. 253
6. Letter to Pollet, 5.2.33. Tyrtaeus (fl. 650 BC) was one of the first ancient poets to use elegiac poetry in war songs.
7. Letter to Grant Richards, 24.7.18, MS University of Illinois: 'I think it best not to make any alterations, even the slightest, after one has printed a thing. It was Shelley's plan, and is much wiser than Wordsworth's perpetual tinkering, as it makes the public fancy one is inspired.' *Letters*, p. 49.
8. It has given its name to a Pre-cambrian rock – *Longmyndian*.
9. John, ch. 3, v. 7 and 8.
10. David Tinkler.
11. The last verse of 'Ha'nacker Mill' runs:

> Spirits that call and no one answers;
> Ha'nackers down and England's done.
> Wind and Thistle for pipe and dancers
> And never a ploughman under the Sun.
> Never a ploughman. Never a one.

12. Letter to H. Martin, 14.4.34, *A.E.H.*, p. 195: 'One version is drunkenest.'
13. In fact spelt 'Onny', a minor mistake of Housman's.
13. It is doubtful whether Housman was referring to the beneficial effects of water, as opposed to alcohol, on the *liver*.
14. Vincent Waite, *Shropshire Hill Country* (Dent, 1970. Republ. Phillimore, 1989).
15. Robert Lynd, Introduction to Mary Webb, *Seven for a Secret* (Cape, 1922).
16. Walter de la Mare, Introduction to Mary Webb, *Poems and Spring of Joy* (Cape, 1928).
17. Edmund Wilson, *The Triple Thinkers* (OUP, 1938), pp. 83–99.
18. Ibid.
19. Written before 1910 but after ASL's publication.
20. Macaulay, 'The Spanish Armada'.

6 · VALEDICTION: THE GREAT TRUTHS

'Please don't kill me,' said the songbird. 'If you will set me free, I'll tell you these three great truths. They will be worth far more to you than a pie for dinner.'
(Aesop's Fable of the Farmer and the Nightingale)

And seek the truth in the groves of Academus
(Horace, Epistles II, ii, 45)

The faintest of all human passions is the love of truth.
(A. E. Housman)[1]

To destroy delusions, as Housman argued in London during the Introductory Lecture of 1892, may regrettably destroy the happiness that the delusion has been cosseting. The truths he plays out in the music of his verses are, therefore, not surprisingly unhappy. Housman was particularly vociferous because of his state of unrequited passion but he was not resentful towards his beloved: the fault was in being homosexual – one of the 'primal faults' as he termed it. Indeed we find him nurturing compassionate thoughts about the same kind of unhappiness in others which fostered what Francis Thompson called 'the sadness in the sweet'[2] in love poems. To be capable of this required the ability to grasp reality while exercising what is called 'a heart'.

True, he wrote poetry when he was physically 'out of sorts', and not the other way around. Apart from needing time away from work to concentrate on composing verse, emotional upset can manifest itself in

visible, physiological ways. In 1933, in his highly controversial and most influential of all public lectures, he
attributed poetical inspiration to the physical effect of a
turbulence in the nervous system; in others the same
process might rather have induced a nervous break-
down, or at the very least complete loss of appetite. In
Housman's case such a process – set in train on hearing
of Moses Jackson's fatal illness – led a man of over sixty
to write fifty-seven pages of poetry between 30 March
and 9 April 1922.

The time he spent studying and correcting the
Classics – which was most of the time – might well have
acted for him in a positive way as a prophylactic against
an outflow of emotion into the medium of his poetry.
Poetry, for him, was induced by emotion not thought.
This was the spearhead of his 1933 oration. Nevertheless, it should be re-emphasised that Housman was not
unusual in taking immense pains to impose discipline
on 'refining' poems which were not satisfactory upon
their initial, emotional release. Tempering his passion
with reason and a feeling for and economy of language,
which is the hallmark of the classicist, he was compassionate at heart, as this poem clearly explains:

> They say my verse is sad: no wonder;
> Its narrow measure spans
> Tears of eternity, and sorrow,
> Not mine, but man's.

> This is for all ill-treated fellows
> Unborn and unbegot,
> For them to read when they're in touble
> And I am not.

> (MP Prefatory Poem)

Housman's gaze is so exclusively directed at despair that it is to his concerns, fundamental truths, that

we must now turn to appreciate his poems. When teaching His truths Jesus Christ used simple language, in parables about ordinary people such as ploughmen and those working in vineyards. Housman wished to attain virtue by distinction, by good conduct and finding the truth; Christ attained virtue by love and teaching love, above all other lessons. It was AD 343 before Prudentius, the first Christian Roman poet we know about, was born. While it was 411 BC when the great Greek Sophist Protagoras (who professed to teach neither science nor scholarship but conduct), was impeached for having written; 'Regarding the gods, I am unable to know whether they exist or do not exist', Prudentius was to find an idea, a faith, that has proved excellent. We know him best for his hymns written because of his religious fervour.

Birth, Love, Nature and Death: these are the topics that have always inspired great poetry, and, while we praise God in his Heaven, the theme of earthly Arcadia has been haunted by all four subjects from classical Greek times. It has persisted in European art, just as in every generation there have been those, too, who looked back on the lost innocence of a past generation, while, in poetry, it expresses itself most movingly in the lyrical, elegiac form, and wields nostalgia as its most powerful weapon.

In his treatment of Nature, as we now know, Housman treats 'wind', for instance, as the metaphoric wind to which poets resort to restore, to wake, to stir up, to calm, and even to revive:

> But from my grave across my brow
> Plays no wind of healing now . . .
>
> (ASL XXX)

While 'exiled' Housman experiences physical pain as

the wind of nostalgia blows into his heart (ASL XL). Life was not meant to be easy: as Housman put it, thinking of the Garden of Eden, 'the tree of man was never quiet', a line which resulted from his notion about the 'primal fault'. To vivify this he has 'the old wind in the old anger' blowing through the woods, bending the 'saplings double' (ASL XXXI).

Nature acts as a mere echo to Housman's lad's troubles; the Wrekin's 'fleece' of wood may heave in the gale, but it was 'the gale of life' which was the subject of the poem. A stranger to Shropshire would learn nothing from this poem about the shape or character of the Wrekin, a formidable, isolated volcanic hump, that can be seen from almost every piece of high ground in the county. Housman was interested in flowers and hedgerows and 'the progress of the seasons' but, as we saw earlier, the Shropshire of *A Shropshire Lad* was a semblance rather than a real place.

Certainly death, and soldiers, are recurring 'Great Subjects' for Housman. He wrote of the tragedy of birth that began for the 'unbegot' the 'rusted wheel of things' all over again. Similiar to the 'paths of glory' of which Gray spoke, Housman follows very different paths that 'lead but to the grave'. Housman translated Horace's thoughts on the cycle of change (Ode iv, 7) in 'Diffugere Nives' (MP V) where, as in Housman, there is sadness of ideas without, somehow, involving gloomy poetry:

> Come *we* where Tullus and where Ancus are,
> And good Aeneas, we are dust and dreams.

Although he hardly worked on Greek authors after 1892 when he became a professor of Latin, Housman did make useful corrections to Greek texts such as to the Athenian dramatic poet Menander (who wrote: 'He whom the gods love dies young'). Menander also wrote a poem we call 'Vanitas Vanitatum' which, having had us peering into the tombs of kings, tyrants, wise, proud and handsome men and found just bones and dust, ends:

All mortals come to the same death.
Look at these and learn what you are yourself.

This in fact is the inscription that Arcadian shepherds are puzzling over as they lean against the tomb. Housman's advice for posterity is:

Dust's your wages, son of sorrow,
But men may come to worse than dust.

(ASL XLIV)

Reputation, which Housman (like Othello) valued above all else, is a laudable death-defying thing. 'Nescit vox missa reverti' (*The voice sent forth cannot be recalled*), he added to the title page of his 1892 lecture before it was published in 1893. There is a hint here of Horace's 'Et semel emissum volat irrevocabile verbum' (*Once a word has been allowed to escape, it cannot be recalled*). But he felt not the slightest misgiving about exposing his poetry to the judgement of posterity.

'My chief object in publishing my verses was to give pleasure to a few young men here and there, and I am glad if they have given pleasure to you', he wrote in 1903[3] to a twenty-two-year-old American poet and playwright. W. H. Auden in 1972 remembered of Housman: 'I don't know how it is with the young today, but to my generation no other English poet seemed so perfectly to express the sensibility of a male adolescent.' But it was not in his character to invite disparaging comment for poor scholarly work – he tore up one lecture as he gave it – or even the kind of stain on his good name had it been learned that he read pornography.

It is not all death and decay that our poet gives adolescents. For variety Housman inserts between dour poems a bracing or (relatively) lighthearted one; he wrote that XX was 'only put in for variety'.[4] The two stanzas of XL and later XLV are wedged between longer poems and each enhance these areas of different moods. In *Last Poems*, Housman groups together a run of three brief, epigrammatic poems, each of two four-line stanzas, between longer, more sombre poems. He does the same twice in *A Shropshire Lad*. The seemingly effortless flow of his syntax is itself immensely varied. No poems adjoin which are identical in form. Even when they do have the same rhythms, the rhyming pattern is different.

His self-criticism was so powerful that he could strike out a verse in order to heighten the impact of a poem. This he did in the poem 'Eight o'Clock' (LP XV), omitting from the published version a third stanza he had written for it. In one of his Notebooks there is an instance of his trying six different words to fit: 'It *tossed* them down.'[5] In 1933 he said that one stanza of the last poem in *A Shropshire Lad* (LXIII) had to be consciously composed 'and that was a laborious business. I wrote it thirteen times, and it was more than a twelvemonth before I got it right'. (The order too would be found if the 'difficult' stanza was discovered.) The flow of that poem never wavers and, like all good songs, it is concise, its rhythm exact and smooth, its rhyming pattern clear. It is not an intellectual experience to read it: the iambics roll out in a sensuous, wistful way unheeded by even a single trochee.

Housman's own style, a kind of concise Anglo-Latinism, led to the brave use of the spondee if one chooses to stress it thus. It is, after all, up to the reader to select how best to read lines like:

> 'What sound awakened me, I wonder,
> For now 'tis dumb.'
> 'Wheels on the road most like, or thunder:
> Lie down; 'twas not the drum.'
>
> (LP XIII)

or these hexameters from ASL:

> Ay, look: high heaven and earth ail from the prime
>   foundation;
> All thoughts to rive the heart are here, and all are
>   vain:
> Horror and scorn and hate and fear and
>   indignation –
> Oh why did I awake? when shall I sleep again?
>
> (ASL XLVIII)

This way of starting a line emphatically is common in Housman's verse. And again we encounter Housman's preference for monosyllables, which also stems from his association with Latin and his liking for making a point succinctly and effectively. It was something Housman was famed for in his 'table talk' at Cambridge. This is the last stanza from LP XXVI where all but three of the fifty-four words in the entire poem are monosyllables:

> I know not if it rains, my love,
> In the land where you do lie;
> And oh, so sound you sleep, my love,
> You know no more than I.

There is simplicity, too, in the last line of the following from ASL XXXIII:

If truth in hearts that perish
Could move the powers on high,
I think the love I bear you
Should make you not to die.

'Religion gives patience', Dr Johnson advised, but atheists like Housman had to devise their own codes of conduct:

June suns, you cannot store them
To warm the winter's cold,
The lad that hopes for heaven
Shall fill his mouth with mould.

(MP XXII)

We shall never know how close Housman was brought to suicide in the autumn of 1885, after Moses and he 'had words', but the following poem, written after 1885, is bitterly ironical in its sense of disharmony with Nature and the world around him. Housman refuses to resort to the 'pathetic fallacy', so characteristic of Mary Webb, whereby Nature is sad or glad in tune with our griefs or joys. Note also the shadow cast by Gray's *Elegy* ('leaves the world to darkness and to me') – or is it Job? – across the first two stanzas:

The world goes none the lamer,
For ought that I can see,
Because this cursed trouble
Has struck my days and me.

The stars of heaven are steady,
The founded hills remain,
Though I to earth and darkness
Return in blood and pain.

Farewell to all belongings
I won or bought or stole;
Farewell, my lusty carcase,
Farewell, my aery soul.

Oh worse remains for others,
And worse to fear had I
Than here at four-and-twenty
To lay me down and die.

(MP XXI)

Over three-quarters of the words are monosyllables, and this accentuates the sense of isolation – without self-pity. The matter-of-fact expression enhances the grief, making it more stark. Equally unfanciful is 'For my Funeral (MP XLVII) – which it was. Enjoying as he did the rhythms of light-hearted music-hall songs, Housman dips such dancing metres into his grief and serves them up stiffened and, as in 'The True Lover' (ASL LIII), still dripping with blood.

In *More Poems*, poems numbered XXX and XXI, above, were about the separation and despair occasioned by the rift with Moses; XLI and XLII were for Adalbert, Moses's brother, while XLVIII mourned for his mother's death and affirmed his loss of faith. When Andrea, his gondolier, died he wrote XLIV, with the sexual symbolism of its ending. It was written in muted but real anguish, although he would also have been experiencing nostalgia for Venice, which in the event he was never to visit again. In its stolid iambic metre it surges pleasantly enough, until the moment comes for the announcements at its *dénouement*:

It looks to north and south,
It looks to east and west;
It guides to Lido mouth
The steersman of Triest.

Andrea, fare you well;
Venice, farewell to thee.
The tower that stood and fell
Is not rebuilt in me.

It is somewhat surprising that, extracted from
among the morbid quality of so much of Housman's
poetry, enough stirring material was to be found for
presentation, as *Selected Poems*[6] to the American Armed
Forces in 1945. This book was designed to arouse valour
in the young soldier's breast; yet MP XXXVII would
rather have struck panic into that breast, were it recited
on the eve of battle. Our fascination with brilliant
artists, musicians, scientists, writers or athletes is
greatly intensified if they die young. Housman never
actually says 'Lads, you're wanted. Come and die.' (last
line of *Recruiting*, by E. A. Mackintosh). But that he
meant as much is strongly suggested. And it is fellow-
feeling rather than pity he is feeling here as he sees
them march off to die:

I wish one could know them, I wish there were tokens
    to tell
The fortunate fellows that now you can never discern;
And then one could talk with them friendly and wish
    them farewell
And watch them depart on the way that they will not
    return.

(ASL XXIII)

Housman applauds the soldier not for winning but for
dying. The glory Housman speaks of is the glory of
young manhood, not of victory. Nor does Housman
seem concerned that, when ordered, a soldier will
fight and kill his nation's foes. The poem ends,

however, with great dignity:

But now you may stare as you like and there's nothing
    to scan;
And brushing your elbow unguessed-at and not to
    be told
They carry back bright to the coiner the mintage
    of man,
The lads that will die in their glory and never be old.

(ASL XXIII)

As for the plight of women in the 1900s – for instance, the suffragette movement or the grief of young widows – Housman seems absolutely uninterested. Yet the letter[7] to his sister Kate, to whom he was devoted, written when one of her sons, Clement, was killed in the trenches, ends in commiseration for 'the poor young girl' who was engaged to Clement. It is even more revealing to read in this letter that Housman had never forgotten what Clement had said to his mother: '. . . I remember you telling me at the beginning of the war that he had almost a hope and expectation of dying in battle.' He enclosed his poem '*Illic Jacet*' (LPIV) (first published in a periodical, *The Academy*, in 1900) 'because the essential business of poetry . . . is to harmonise the sadness of the universe, and it is somehow more sustaining and healing than prose', and because of the idea that 'lads are in love with the grave'. His portrayal of women and girls in *A Shropshire Lad* is generally as passive receptacles for the 'lads': they are often treated as part of the romantic Arcadian idyll, as though Housman is not able to see them directly but only at one remove, as an appendage to the lads. They exist only in so far as they enhance the manhood of his young men, or embellish the backdrop of the Arcadian setting:

> The rose-lipt girls are sleeping
> In fields where roses fade.
>
> (ASL LIV)

Housman liked to use the word 'rose' as a metaphor for the 'deplorable sex'.[8] There is a certain inevitability that it was 'Rose Harland' who was, it is to be supposed, 'Terence Hearsay's' girlfriend, at any rate after her 'Fred' had died:

> When Rose and I walk out together
> Stock-still lies Fred and sleeps.
>
> (ASL XXV)

If one can read without discomposure 'To an Athlete Dying Young' (ASL XIX) one can see how Housman evokes the image of the evergreen laurel: since the days of ancient Greece it has been for poets the reward of champions and the emblem of immortality. However, once cut, laurel quickly turns grey and stiffens up. It lasts for a very long time in its dried state, as it would in a victor's crown preserved well after the death of its recipient. This then is Housman's metaphor for a lad who dies young. The rose, which can in contrast stay fresh for many months in a vase, is his metaphor for a girl, even for an athlete's girlfriend who lives on after her lover's death though she cannot achieve immortality as he does:

> Smart lad, to slip betimes away
> From fields where glory does not stay
> And early though the laurel grows
> It withers quicker than the rose.
>
> (ASL XIX)

(Moses Jackson had been a champion runner, and Housman had seen the prize cups when they shared rooms in London.) Housman knew and loved Swinburne's musical line 'Shall I strew on thee rose or rue or laurel'[9], but these lines exemplify an especial degree of subtlety in Housman's poetry. It is an old trick; the juxtaposition of laurels against roses almost certainly arose as a classical allusion such as first seen in the writings of the stoic Epictetus.[10]

The last words in *A Shropshire Lad* – whether Terence Hearsay's or Housman's – are not worthy of being inscribed in bright golden letters, or of being shouted from tops of roofs or Wrekin's summit. They epitomise all that is forlorn, albeit generous-spirited, in Housman. They make their appearance as little more than a muted echo:

> And fields will yearly bear them
> As light-leaved spring comes on,
> And luckless lads will wear them
> When I am dead and gone.
>
> (ASL LXIII)

Can one not hear the silence?

There is no poem more sad than Sappho's single line: 'I loved thee once, Athis, long ago.' To span an ocean with love, and to keep a dream alive for over fifty years, is a feat of loving, especially if it is one-sided. In truth, most of Housman's poems were for Moses Jackson. The strength of his devotion is proved by Housman's taking the for him unprecedented step of dedicating Volume I of *Manilius* to Jackson. Thwarted of his mother's love when she died on his twelfth birthday, he was later to be denied Moses as well. Housman chose to map his grief alone. In exploring the many forms of unrequited love and elegising his 'land of lost content',

Housman was giving vent to primal feelings not just for one other fellow human, but for a whole world that was irretrievably gone – his own personal Arcadia. Such reverie has struck chords in all readers who look back on the innocence of their childhood as a lost paradise, while, for many young men, as Dr Johnson put it, 'The Shepherd in Virgil grew at last acquainted with love, and found him a native of the rocks.'

The most fitting epitaph for Housman would be a Latin one, appropriately by his favourite Roman poet, Propertius: 'Qui nunc iacet horrida pulvis, unicus hic quondam servus amoris erat' (*He that now lies naught but unlovely dust, once served love and one love only*).

NOTES

1. Quoted in A.E. Housman: *Selected Prose* ed. John Carter (CUP, 1969).
2. From *Daisy*.
3. Letter to W. Bynner, 3.6.03, MS Harvard.
4. Letter to J.W. Mackail, 25.7.22, MS Trinity.
5. *A.E.H.*, p. 253. Laurence also says that 'rive' was reacted after 8 tries in ASL XLVIII.
6. Housman, *Selected Poems* (H. Holt, 1945).
7. Letter to Katharine Symons, 5.10.15, MS Lilly.
8. Housman's term as quoted by Laurence in *The Unexpected Years* (Cape 1937).
9. Swinburne: 'Ave atque Vale' – addressed to Baudelaire. In a letter to Edmund Gosse, 9.4.17, who had just published a life of Swinburne, Housman wrote: 'It rejoices me to find that the only two things I ever admired in (Swinburne's) later volumes – "Ave atque Vale" itself and the prologue to "Tristram"'. MS British Museum.
10. Robert Graves in *The White Goddess* describes the hallucinogenic properties of laurel. He describes how the female celebrants of the Triple Moon Goddess at Tempe in

northern Thessaly used to chew laurel leaves as an hallu-
cinogen so as to attain a state of erotic frenzy. Every ninth
year a sacred mission would go to the Vale of Temple in
order to pluck laurel for the victors' wreaths at the forth-
coming Pythian Games.

POSTSCRIPT

In August 1987 I met a middle-aged West Staffordshire
man who one might call a 'white-collar worker' and 'a
hard grafter'. Though he had no idea what his wife read
on her side of the bed, he told me that he always kept
Housman's *A Shropshire Lad* and *Collected Poems* by his
bedside. He told me that he knew all the poems by
heart. In fact, he said that he always spent the last ten
minutes of every evening reading Housman. On long
car journeys he even preferred to recite these poems to
listening to the radio. The reason for this devotion, he
confided, was that he had done his courting in Ludlow
and come across *A Shropshire Lad* there; now he returned to the trysting place once every month, simply
for the pleasure of being there and on the hills in
the company of his wife. He found lasting stimulation
in continually reading Housman's most 'descriptive
poetry', by which I assume him to have meant all the
arcadian passages as well as the Ludlow poems.

I asked him whether he did not find *A Shropshire
Lad* just a bit maudlin. Haltingly, he replied that it was
the simplicity of the poems and the description of
natural beauty that had won him over. I hope my book
will speed him on his journey back to Arcadia, and
inspire others to seek, even in their imagination, such
places. For it is a quest which, becoming for everyone
everywhere more and more difficult, must never be
given up.

SELECT BIBLIOGRAPHY

Brink, C. O., *English Classical Scholarship: Historical Reflections on Bentley, Porson and Housman* (James Clarke & Co., Cambridge, and OUP, New York, 1986).

Dolenski, Leo and Dooley, John, *The Name and Nature of A. E. Housman* (Bryn Mawr, 1986).

Gow, A. S. F., *A. E. Housman: A Sketch* (Cambridge University Press, 1936). Best for lists of Housman's classical writings and his years at Trinity.

Graves, Richard Perceval, *A. E. Housman: The Scholar-Poet* (Routledge & Kegan Paul). A most readable biography.

Haber, Tom Burns, *A. E. Housman* (Twayne series, 1967).

—— *The Manuscript Poems of A. E. Housman* (OUP, 1955).

Hawkins, Maude M., *Man Behind a Mask* (Chicago University Press, 1958).

Housman, A. E., *The Collected Poems of A. E. Housman*, with an excellent introduction by John Sparrow (Penguin, 1956).

—— *The Classical Papers of A. E. Housman*, ed. J. Diggle and F. R. D. Goodyear (CUP, 1972).

—— *A. E. Housman: Collected Poems and Selected Prose*, ed. with admirable introduction by Christopher Ricks (Allen Lane and the Penguin Press 1988).

—— *A. E. Housman: Selected Prose* (Cambridge University Press, 1961. Ed. John Carter. Includes texts of 1892 and 1933 lectures.

—— *The Confines of Criticism*, Cambridge Inaugural Lecture, 1911, with notes by John Carter (Cambrige University Press, 1969).

—— *The Letters of A. E. Housman*, ed. Henry Maas (Hart-Davis and Granada, 1971). Contains about 850 letters, including a small second section of letters on classical subjects. Two hundred and eight letters are to his publisher – though many more were available in the Adelman Collection at Bryn Mawr.

Housman, Laurence, *The Unexpected Years* (Bobbs-Merrill, 1936; Cape, 1937). Best, as it should be, for Housman's early life and Clemence Housman's *The Were-Wolf* and anecdotes.

—— *A. E. H.: Some Poems, Some Letters and a Personal Memoir by his Brother* (Cape, 1937). Good for early life, photographs, letters, *Additional Poems*, and detailed chronology of poems from Housman's Notebooks.

—— 'A. E. Housman's "De Amicitia"', annotated by John Carter, *Encounter* (Oct. 1967). Original in British Library.

Lucas, F. L. '"Fool's errand to the Grave": the Personality and Poetry of Housman'. In F. L. Lucas, *The Greatest Problem* (1961). Has been called 'The best critical account' (H. Maas, in his Bibliography of *The Letters of A. E. Housman*.

Manilius, *Astronomica*, trans. G. P. Goold, Loeb Classical Library edn (Heineman, 1977). A prose translation.

Marlow, Norman, *A. E. Housman: Scholar and Poet* (Routledge & Kegan Paul, 1958).

Page, Norman *A. E. Housman: A Critical Biography* (Schocken Books, 1983). An intelligent study.

Pugh, John, *Bromsgrove and the Housmans* (Housman Society, 1974). Mr Pugh has done much to revive interest in Housman through editing the *Housman Journal* – and organising the making of Housman's life-size statue in Bromsgrove High Street.

Richards, Grant, *Housman: 1897–1936* (OUP, 1941; Octagon Books, 1973).

Ricks, Christopher (ed.), *A. E. Housman: A Collection of Critical Essays* (Prentice-Hall, 1968). Fascinating academic and not so academic cricitism.

Sparrow, John, *Housman Obscured: Independent Essays* (Faber, 1963). Sparrow's appreciation for Housman makes this a rewarding study.

Symons, Katharine E. *et al.*, *A. E. Housman: Recollections and Reflections* (New York, 1937).

Watson, George L., *A. E. Housman: A Divided Life* (Hart-Davis, 1957).

Withers, Percy, *A Buried Life* (Cape, 1940).

ILLUSTRATED EDITIONS OF *A SHROPSHIRE LAD*

George G. Harrap first published, in 1940, a very popular edition illustrated with black-and-white wood engravings by Agnes Miller Parker. This is now in its tenth edition.

My own illustrated edition was published in 1988 by Ashford.